CHINESE QIGONG
SERIES 4

THREE-BATH QIGONG

三浴氣功

HAI FENG PUBLISHING CO., LTD. 海峰出版社

© **Hai Feng Publishing Co., Ltd.**
ISBN 962-238-152-9

Copy Editor
Liu Yu Xizn

Published by
Hai Feng Publishing Co., Ltd.
Rm. 1502, Wing On House,
71 Des Voeux Road, Central,
Hong Kong

Printed by
Lammar Offset Printing Ltd.
Flat C, 16/F, Aik Sun Factory Bldg.,
14 Westland Rd., Quarry Bay,
Hong Kong

Second Edition March 1998

責任編輯
劉玉仙

出版
海峰出版社
香港中環德輔道中71號
永安集團大廈1502室

印刷
藍馬柯式印務有限公司
香港鰂魚涌華蘭路十四號
益新工業大廈16字樓C座

一九九八年三月第二版

HF-126-P

CONTENTS

Three-Bath Qigong

Three-Bath Qigong

Yang Guoquan

I. Characteristics of Three-Bath Qigong

1. Definition

Three-Bath Qigong is for heatlth-care of the old and the middle-aged people.

It shall be taken every morning in the sun at places with fresh air, for instance, lakeside and riverside. The three baths refer to the sun, water, and air baths.

2. Features

(1) The exercise is beneficial to all parts of the body.

(2) With medium strenuity, it is suited to the physiological functioning of the old and the middle-aged people, and becomes an effective means for prevention and cure of diseases and promotion of heatlth.

(3) The four sets of the exercise can be done completely or partially.

(4) The exercise has no special requirements on outfits, environment, and climate. It is good for all people, male and female, the old-aged and the middle-aged, the strong and the weak.

3. Essentials

(1) Get rid of all distracting thoughts and concentrate on the exercise to lead the movements with your mind. That is, to combine the mind with the vital energy and strength.

(2) Breathe gently, evenly and slowly. Inhale and exhale as much as you can. Use abdominal breathing (through nose, with abdominal wall protruded when inhaling and retracted when exhaling), and keep your mind on *Dantian*, a point three *Cun* (9.9 cm) below the navel.

(3) Relax every part of your body. Use moderate force and speed.

(4) Proceed with correct posture and rhythm, and alternate tension with relaxation.

4. Points for attention

(1) Rinse your mouth after getting up and take some lukewarm water before doing the exercise.

(2) Do not do the exercise in dirty air. When it is cold, breathe slowly and shallowly. Do not breathe deeply in smoke and fog.

(3) In cold winter, the first set, the health-care massage, can be done indoors after rising up or before going to bed. It can also be done in bed.

(4) The exercise shall be suited to individual cases. Patients with chronic diseases shall be exempt from the exercise during attack. Patients during recovery shall increase the intensity in accordance with their physical condition. Patients suffering hypertension, coronary heart disease, cerebral arteriosclerosis, and lung disorders shall use less force.

(5) Do it everyday and in all weather.

5. Effects

Three-Bath Qigong helps patients to recover, the weak to become strong, and healthy persons to prolong life.

II. Names of the Movements

First Set   Preliminaries – Health-Care Massage
1. Clear Heart and Tonify Brain
2. Knead Eyes and Scrub Face
3. Knead *Taiyang* Acupoint
4. Bathe Nose against Cold
5. Beat Drum and Rub Ears
6. Knock Teeth and Rinse Mouth
7. Rub and Turn Neck
8. Push Abdomen to Regulate Intestines
9. Scrub Kidneys to Strengthen Loins
10. Stroke Legs and Bend Toes

Second Set   Principal Exercise – Upper Part
1. White Crane Spreads Wings
2. Tiger Lunges at Prey
3. White Ape Offers Peaches
4. Wind Sweeps Leaves
5. Pointing the Way
6. Dragons Coil round Pillar
7. Fish Moon from Sea
8. Looking into Distance
9. Caring the Lung
10. Horse-Ride Breathing

Third Set   Principal Exercise – Middle Part
1. Swan Soars into Sky
2. Tightening Bow
3. Spread Chest to Tone Lung
4. Pick Moon and Star
5. Hug Moon
6. Look Right and Left
7. The Pillar
8. Gyrate Hips and Push Loins
9. Golden Rooster Stands on One Leg
10. Turn and Bend Knees

Fourth Set   Principal Exercise – Lower Part
1. Hold the Sky
2. Draw the Bow
3. Raise Hand to Fix Spleen
4. Look Back to Regulate Vital Energy
5. Glare and Thrust Fists
6. Touch Feet to Fix Kidney
7. Wag Tail to Strengthen Heart
8. Ride a Horse and Swing
9. Eyes Follow Swinging Hand
10. Roc Spreads Wings

III. Explanations of the Movements

First Set   Preliminaries — Health-Care Massage
Commencing stance: Stand erect, relax your mind and body, part your feet to width of the shoulders, and grasp the ground with your toes.

1. Clear Heart and Tonify Brain
Movements: (1) Rub scalp: Place left hand on the forehead, and right hand on the occipital bone. Rub the scalp with both hands right and left with moderate force for 16 times (Fig. 1).

(2) Scratch scalp: With tips of th ten fingers, scratch the scalp up and down in three layers, beginning from the front, for twice (Fig. 2).

(3) Stroke scalp: Palms press the forehead and stroke back along the scalp 8 times (Fig. 3).

Essentials: Keep your mind on *Baihui* on top of the head, use moderate force, and breathe naturally.

Effects: Regulating functioning of the nerves, tonifying brain, invigorating the scalp, and protecting the hair.

Fig. 1 Rubbing scalp.

Fig. 2 Scratching scalp.

Fig. 3 Stroking scalp.

8

2. Knead Eyes and Scrub Face

Movements: (1) Knead eyes: Close eyes slightly and knead eyeballs with hypothenar of the palms leftward in 16 circles, rightward in 16 circles, horizontally for 16 times and up and down for 16 times (Figs. 4 and 5).

(2) Scrub face: Start to scrub face with palms from the forehead, down to the chin and up to the ears. Rub helixes with thumbs and forefingers up to top of the head and back to the forehead. Eight times. (Fig. 6)

(3) Turn eyes: Close eyes slightly, turn eyeballs in 16 left circles. Slowly open eyes and stare into distance for a while. Repeat the movement but in 16 right circles (Fig. 7).

Essentials: Keep your mind on the two eyes. Use even force, and turn eyeballs slowly. Do no wink while staring.

Effects: Smoothing facial skin, and preventing eye diseases of the old and middle-aged people.

Fig. 4 Kneading eyes.

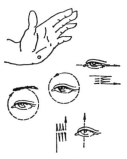

Fig. 5 Location of eye-kneading.

Fig. 6 Scrubbing face.

Fig. 7 Turning eyes.

3. Knead *Taiyang* Acupoint

Movements: (1) Knead *Taiyang*: With the four fingers closed, the thumbs press heavily on *Taiyang* on both sides. Place second knuckle of forefingers lightly on *Zanshu*, and turn inward in a circle and then outward, each 16 times (Fig. 8).

(2) Stroke eyebrows: Fix thumbs on *Taiyang*, and stroke with second knuckle of forefingers from *Tianmu* in the forehead to *Taiyang*, 16 times (Fig. 9).

Essentials: Keep your mind on *Taiyang*. Close eyes, and use light and even force.

Effects: Clearing eyes, regulating functioning of the nerves and preventing hardening of cerebral arteries and eye diseases among the aging.

Fig. 8 Kneading *Taiyang*.

Fig. 9 Stroking eyebrows.

4. Bathe Nose against Cold

Movements: With fingers slightly bent, rub the nose with back of thumbs along the two sides of the nasal bone from *Yingxiang* by the nostrils up to corner of eyes, and down, 16 times. Use thumb knuckles and knead *Yingxiang* in inward and outward circles, each 16 times (Figs. 10 and 11).

Essentials: Keep your mind on *Yingxiang.*

Effects: Preventing and curing cold, rhinitis, nasosinusities, and facial paralysis.

5. Beat Drum and Rub Ears

Movements: (1) Beat drum: Cover ears tightly with palms, and lightly drum the occipital bone with the three fingers in the middle, 16 times (Fig. 12).

(2) Rub ears: Continued from the previous posture. Fix fingers on occipital bone, and jerk palms off ears after pressing them hard. Sixteen times.

Essentials: Keep your mind on *Naohu* whne beating the occipital bone to hear a drumming sound. When rubbing ears, keep your mind on the drum heads, and use moderate force with mouth slightly open.

Effects: Clearing the mind, improving memory, protecting hearing, and preventing deafness, tinnitus and other ear diseases among the aging.

Fig. 10 Bathing nose.   Fig. 11 Kneading *Yingxiang.*   Fig. 12 Beating the drum.

6. Knock Teeth and Rinse Mouth

Movements: (1) Knock teeth: Close mouth slightly, with thumbs on lower jaw (*Zengyin*), forefingers on tragi (*Tinggong*), middle fingers on *Taiyang*. Open and close your teeth. Knock gently the front teeth 16 times and then the back teeth, 16 times (Fig. 13).

(2) Rinse mouth: Place tip of tongue against upper jaw and rinse 64 times. Send down the mouthful of saliva in three gulps (Fig. 14).

Essentials: Concentrate on *Xiaguan* when knocking teeth with increasing force, and on tip of tongue when rinsing.

Effects: Strengthening teeth against odontopathy. Gulps of saliva help digestion and protect digestive system.

7. Rub and Turn Neck

Movements: (1) Rub neck: Place hands on back of the neck, hold tendons with thumbs, forefingers and middle fingers, from *Yamen* to *Fengfu*. Stroke the tendons upward with force 16 times, and downward 16 times (Fig. 15). Place left hand on right side of the neck, and right hand on the left, from *Yamen* to the throat, and rub tendons in the neck alternatively 32 times (Fig. 16).

(2) Turn neck: Place right hand over left (the opposite for females), with *Laogong* on each hand overlapping, and press lower *Dantian*. Turn neck clockwise and counter-clockwise, each 8 times (Fig. 17). Bend neck forward and backward, 8 times (Fig. 18).

(3) Smooth channels: Place right hand over left (the opposite for females), with the throat between thumbs and forefingers. Inhale, push the air down to lower *Dantian* with your hands, and raise your heels. Put heels down after inhaling to the full. Exhale, and swing slightly your arms back and forth 4 times. Repeat 4 times (Figs. 19, 20 and 21).

Essentials: Concentrate on *Yamen* when rubbing and turning the neck, and on lower *Dantian* when easing the channels.

Effects: Promoting and smoothing functioning of channels and blood vessels in head and neck, clearing the heart, invigorating the brain and preventing cerebral arteriosclerosis and high blood pressure.

Fig. 13 Knocking teeth.

Fig. 14 Rinsing mouth.

Fig. 15 Rubbing neck.

Fig. 16 Scrubbing tendons in the neck.

Fig. 17 Turning neck.

Fig. 18 Bending neck.

Fig. 19 Smoothing channels.

Fig. 20 Smoothing channels.

Fig. 21 Smoothing channehs.

8. Push Abdomen to Regulate Intestines

Movements: (1) Push abdomen: Move left foot half a step forward to the left, with torso inclining in the same direction. Press palms on hollows below the ribs, and push forward to the navel. Place right hand over the left (the opposite for females) with *Laogong* in each hand overlapping, and push with force to lower *Dantian*. And then rub back up to the ribs. Do it 8 times. Left foot falls back. Do it all over with the right foot for 8 times (Fig. 22).

(2) Regulate intestines: Place right hand over left (the opposite for females), with *Laogong* in each hand overlapping, against the navel. Turn hands clockwise, rubbing and kneading, in 8 small circles, 8 medium circles, and 8 large circles. Change the position of hands (left hand over right) and turn them counterclockwise, rubbing and kneading, in 8 large circles, 8 medium circles and 8 small circles. Return to the commencing stance (Fig. 23).

Essentials: Keep your mind on lower *Dantian*. Increase force gradually. Pregnant women, and people suffering acute abdominal inflammation and tumor are prohibited.

Effects: Regulating functioning of stomach and intestines, helping digestion, preventing and curing stomach and abdominal diseases.

Fig. 22 Pushing abdomen.

Fig. 23 Regulating intestines.

9. Scrub Kidneys to Strengthen Loins

Movements: Place back of hands on both sides of small of the back. Rub heavily down to free end of the sacrum, and back up to as far as you can go. Do it 32 times (Fig. 24).

Essentials: Keep your mind on *Shenshu* in the back.

Effects: Strengthening the loins, invigorating functions of kidney, preventing and curing kidney and lumbar disorders.

10. Stroke Legs and Bend Toes

Movements: (1) Stroke legs and knead knees: Move right leg a step to the right, bend right leg and straighten left leg into a bow stance. Place right palm above right knee, and hold left hip with the thumb and forefinger of left hand. Push heavily along lateral side of leg down to the ankle. Turn to medial side and back up to the base of leg. Stroke diagonally and return to the hip. Eight times. Put left hand on the knee cap, with *Laogong* over upper rim and thumb on *Xuehai* between the thigh and knee joints. Make 8 left turns, and 8 right turns. Raise your body slowly (Fig. 25). Repeat with left bow stance and right hand stroking right leg for 8 times.

Fig. 24 Scrubbing kidneys.

Fig. 25 Stroking leg.

(2) Bend toes: Stand erect. Shift body weight onto right foot, keep left leg straight, and raise left foot forward to the right. Bend toes of left foot up and down to open and close *Yongquan* in the sole. Do it 8 times. Move body weight to the left foot; and repeat with the right foot for 8 times (Fig. 26).

Essentials: Keep your mind on *Zusanyang* and *Zusanyin* while stroking the leg, on *Xuehai* while kneading the knee, and on *Yongquan* while bending toes.

Effects: Leg stroking stimulates blood circulation in lower limbs, smooths functioning of channels, prevents and cures muscular atrophy, varicose vein, dropsy of lower limbs, and gonitis. Toe bending is curative for high blood pressure, stuffy nose, dizziness, cold feet of the aged, and numbness in lower limbs.

Second Set   Principal Exercise – Upper Part

Commencing stance: Same as that for the first set.

1. White Crane Spreads Wings

Movements: Clench hands into loose fists, stretch and raise arms slowly in front, and inhale. Spread fingers after reaching over the head, lower arms sideways, and exhale. As the hands reach down the sides of the body, close your fingers, and swing your arms back and forth once. Do it 8 times (Figs. 27 and 28).

Fig. 26 Bending toes.

Fig. 27 White crane spreads wings.

Fig. 28 White crane spreads wings.

Essentials: Breathe deeply, and drop the vital energy down to lower *Dantian.* Do not raise your heels.

Effects: Removing stagnancy in channels of arms, activitating the heart and lung, speeding up blood circulation, and preventing and curing functional disturbances of shoulder joints.

2. Tiger Lunges at Prey

Movements: Hang down your arms naturally, raise them up and back. When hands come over your head, stretch your body backward as far as you can, and exhale. Lunge forward with your hands, and bring them to the tips of your toes with fingers clenched. Raise your body and inhale. Clench hands into fists, thumbs side up, and raise arms to horizontal position when erecting the torso. Stretch fingers, lower arms, and return to the starting posture. Do it 8 times (Figs. 29 and 30).

Essentials: Do it with ease. Inhale and exhale as much as you can. Lunge forward with large swing of your arms, and straightened legs. Patients with high blood pressure is forbidden when during attack.

Effects: Exercising shoulder and back muscles and tendons, activating lumbar vertebrae and shoulder joints, promoting peristalsis of the stomach and intestines, and preventing and curing elderly people's diseases in the shoulder, back, stomach and intestines.

Fig. 29 Tiger lunges at prey.

Fig. 30 Tiger lunges at prey.

3. White Ape Offers Peaches

Movements: Hang down arms naturally, with palms turning back. Move left foot a step to the left, turn torso to the left. Erect torso, bend it slowly back, and inhale. Straighten left leg, holding the ground with toes, and slightly bend right leg. Raise hands over head in an arc, palms up, fingers pointing back. Stare into the sky. Inhale as much as you can, swing down your arms, and exhale. Place hands in the original position and go back to the starting posture. Reverse right and left. Do it alternately each 16 times (Fig. 31).

Essentials: Bend the torso back into an arch. The body weight is on the side-stepped leg, while the stress is on the back and shoulders. Drop the vital energy down to lower *Dantian*. Relax arms when restoring to original posture.

Effects: Exercising the shoulders, and lumbar and hip joints, expanding the chest, benefiting the diaphragm, removing stagnancy of vital energy of the liver, subduing hyperactivity of the *Yang* (vital function) of the stomach, and preventing and curing elderly people's spinal curvature and lumbargo.

4. Wind Sweeps Leaves

Movements: Makes a big stride to the left with Left foot, straighten and raise arms, palms forward. Bend back your body, and, taking the waist as the axis, move it in slow clockwise circle while exhaling. When body comes to the lowest point, try to touch the ground with finger tips, and exhale as much as you can. Raise arms together with torso to the right and up, and inhale as much as you can. Return arms to original position. Do the circling 8 times. Do 8 counterclockwise circles in the same way (Figs. 32 and 33).

Essentials: Keep your legs straightened, and steady yourself by holding the ground with your toes. The arms shall be kept at shoulder-width, swing in circles as large as possible, and move with the torso. Keep your mind on the void high above.

Effects: Strengthening the back and kidneys, exercising every part of the body, and preventing dizziness.

5. Pointing the Way

Movements: Bend fingers into swords (with forefingers and middle fingers stretched and the other fingers slightly bent), and hang arms by the side. Circle left hand clockwise. When it comes to the highest point, turn palm inward. When it comes to the left, turn palm outward, with eyes following finger tips. When it is coming down to original position, turn right hand counterclockwise. When it comes to the right, finger tips are followed by the eyes. The two hands make 16 alternating circles (Fig. 34).

Essentials: The eyes shall always follow the fingers. Concentrate your mind on the finger swords.

Effects: Exercising the upper limbs, and improving eyesight.

Fig. 31 White ape offers
peaches.

Fig. 32 Wind sweeps leaves.

Fig. 33 Wind sweeps leaves.

Fig. 34 Pointing the way.

6. Dragons Coil round Pillar

Movements: Slightly bend your knees, and clench hands into loose fists. Bend right arm and beat left-side chest. Stretch left arm backward and lightly strike right-side loin. Before returning to the original posture, lightly strike lower abdomen with left palm, and *Mingmen* with the back of right hand. Straighten the legs. Do it 8 times (Figs. 35 and 36). Reverse right and left, and do it 8 times.

Essentials: Keep your mind on *Zhongfu*. Movements of the arms shall be coordinated with bending and stretching of the knees.

Effects: Exercising shoulders, elbows, wrists, and knees. Preventing and curing joint disorders, and pleurisy.

7. Fish Moon from Sea

Movements: Move left foot half a step to the left, and raise straightened arms sideways to horizontal level. Bend down at the waist, and exhale, with arms reaching down in arc and cross fingers forming a scoop. Erect torso, with hands rising above the head. Turn palms downward, fingers of hands pointing to each other. Press hands downward from the chest, inhale, and drop the vital energy to lower *Dantian*. Do it 8 times (Figs. 37, 38 and 39).

Essentials: It is to be done with great ease. Inhale and exhale as much as you can.

Effects: Strenghtening lumbar joints and respiratory muscles, preventing and curing lumbar spurs, pleurisy, and disorders of internal organs.

Fig. 35 Dragons coil round pillar.

Fig. 36 Dragons coil round pillar.

Fig. 37 Fishing moon from sea.

Fig. 38 Fishing moon from sea.

Fig. 39 Fishing moon from sea.

8. Looking into Distance

Movements: Continued from the previous posture. Move left foot another half a step, with arms akimbo. Bend torso to the right while exhaling. When it comes to 90 degrees with the legs, turn left, with waist as the axis. Raise your head while turning, and scan into the distance. When your head comes to the left, erect torso, inhale, and bend torso back, staring into the sky. Inhale to the full, return to the original posture by the same route. Reverse right and left, and do it 8 times (Figs. 40 and 41).

Essentials: Stand fast on your feet, turn slowly, gaze into the distance, and inhale and exhale to the full.

Effects: Regulating eyesight, strengthening the back and lung, preventing and curing near-sightedness, old sightedness, and lacrimation in the wind.

9. Caring the Lung

Movements: Continued from the previous posture. Retrieve left foot one step, with arms akimbo. Turn left shoulder uniformly in up, front, down and back circles. When it comes down, raise right shoulder and turn. Do it 16 times. Stop for a while and begin with the right shoulder. Do another 16 times. Hang your arms by the side and come back to the commencing stance (Fig. 42).

Essentials: Movement of the shoulders promotes activities of the lungs. Keep your waist steady while gyrating shoulders, and your mind on shoulders.

Effects: Activating shoulder joints, and stimulating lung activities to prevent and cure lung disorders.

Fig. 40 Looking into distance.   Fig. 41 Looking into distance.

10. Horse-Ride Breathing

Movements: Continued from the previous posture. Draw in tips of your feet, stretch your arms forward and raise them horizontally. Clench hands into loose fists, thumbs side down. Bend knees into horse-ride stance, and inhale gently. Jerk your body up and down several times, and inhale as much as you can. Straighten knees and exhale. Hang down your arms, swing them gently until you have exhaled. Repeat the exercise once again and return to the commencing stance (Figs. 43 and 44).

Essentials: Keep your torso erect and knees in line with toes. Drop vital energy to lower *Diantian*.

Effects: Exercising lumbar, hip, knee and ankle joints, removing stagnancy of vital energy of the channels to build up physique and preventing and curing backache.

Fig. 42 Caring the lung.

Fig. 43 Horse-ride breathing.

Fig. 44 Horse-ride breathing.

Third Set   Principal Exercise – Middle Part
Commencing stance: Same as that for the first set.

1. Swan Soars into Sky
Movements: (1) Swan soars: Cross arms in front, bend knees slightly, and exhale as much as you can. Straighten your legs, stretch your arms and raise them sideways, and inhale. Hands touch over head with *Laogong* overlapping each other. Lower arms sideways and cross them in front. Eight times (Figs. 45 and 46).

(2) Swan flies: Continued from the previous posture. Swing arms wideways with palms down, and inhale. Swing left leg sideways at the same time, raise right heel. Lower down arms and exhale. Lower left leg. Reverse right and left leg, alternating 16 times (Figs. 47 and 48).

Essentials: The soaring movements are slow and smooth, breathing deeply, gently, and a little bit fast. The flying movements are continuous and relaxed, with your mind concentrating on the void.

Effects: Exercising the joints and muscles of the limbs, regulating the nervou system and coordinating body movement.

2. Tightening Bow
Movements: Continued from the previous posture. Turn palms down in front, raise arms diagonally downward, relax fingers, and inhale. Bend your back slowly but forcefully into a bow. Raise arms from the back to over the head. Erect torso slowly, bend slightly forward, and exhale. Arms return in front to original position. Do it 8 times (Figs. 49 and 50).

Essentials: When curving back, hold the ground with your toes and stand fast. Drop vital energy to lower *Diantian.*

Effects: Promoting smooth circulation of blood and vital energy, exercising the lung, and back and abdominal muscles, preventing and curing old people's spinal curvature.

Fig. 45 Swan soars into sky.

Fig. 46 Swan soars into sky.

Fig. 47 Swan flies.

Fig. 48 Swan flies.

Fig. 49 Tightening bow.

Fig. 50 Tightening bow.

3. Spread Chest to Tone Lung

Movements: Continued from the previous posture. Curve fingers, bend torso to 90 degrees, draw in chest, and exhale. Stretch arm as if scrooping something, while exhaling to the full. Erect torso slowly, arms following, and inhale. When torso becomes upright, expand chest by moving arms sideways down, and arch torso. When hands come to the lowest point, inhale as much as you can. Do it 8 times (Figs. 51, 52 and 53).

Essentials: Expand the chest in slow movement with feet standing fast. Drop vital energy to lower *Diantian*.

Effects: Extending chest, exercising respiratory muscles and strengthening the heart and lung.

Fig. 51 Spreading chest to tone lung.

Fig. 52 Spreading chest to tone lung.

Fig. 53 Spreading chest to tone lung.

4. Pick Moon and Stars

Movements: Arms akimbo, move left foot a step forward to form left bow stance. Turn torso to the left and hang down left arm, with fingers spreading out. Raise it in an arc. When it comes over the head, close the five fingers. Twist left arm and turn it backward to original place. Spread fingers. Do it 16 times (Fig. 54). Straighten legs and turn torso to the front. Turn left hand from lower left to upper right, and inhale. When the hand is over head, clasp the fingers and return hand by original route, and exhale. Spread fingers with palm backward. Do it 16 times. Reverse right and left and do the exercise 16 times (Figs. 55 and 56).

Essentials: Keep your mind on the fingers. Eyes follow fingers.

Effects: Exercing shoulders, elbows, wrists, and fingers. Preventing and curing tremor and numbness in terminals of the limbs, and omarthritis.

Fig. 54 Picking moon and stars.

Fig. 55 Picking moon and stars.

Fig. 56 Picking moon and stars.

5. Hug Moon

Movements: Continued from the previous posture. Hold an imaginary ball in your hands, with *Laogong* opposite to each other. Push hands in an arc toward upper left. Torso follows hands and lunges toward left. Lift right heel, shift body weight onto left leg. Reverse right and left, alternating 8 times (Fig. 57).

Essentials: Keep your mind on *Laogng.* Eyes follow hands in flowing movement. Push your hands, as if holding ball, as far as you can, with medium force.

Effects: Exercising limb and body muscles, strengthening the heart, and building up physique.

6. Look Right and Left

Movements: Continued from the previous posture. Retrieve left foot half a step, a little more than the shoulders' width from the right foot, arms akimbo. Bend torso slowly forward to 90 degrees, and exhale. Bob torso 4 times. Exhale to the full and raise torso. While inhaling bend torso to the left, raise rigth arm sideways to over head and bend elbow with palm up, looking at left heel. Bob torso to lower left 4 times. Inhale as much as you can. Torso returns to upright position with arms akimbo. Reverse right and left, and alternate 4 times. Return to the commencing stance (Figs. 58 and 59).

Essentials: Use gentle force when bending the torso. Keep knees straightened. Drop vital energy to lower *Dantian.*

Effects: Exercising flank and lumbar muscles, and strengthening spleen and stomach.

Fig. 57 Hugging moon.

7. The Pillar

Movements: Continued from the previous posture. Stretch up torso with arms akimbo, raise heels, and inhale. Turn palms down with fingers pointing forward, and press. Heels ram on the ground, and exhale to the full. Do it 8 times (Figs. 60, 61 and 62).

Essentials: Stretch torso up with force. Drop vital energy to lower *Dantian.* Ram heels on ground with force to feel percussions in the head.

Effects: Stretching ligamenta of the whole body, normalizing circulation of vital energy, invigorating the pulse-beat, building up physique, and tonifying the brain.

Fig. 58 Looking right and left.

Fig. 59 Looking right and left.

Fig. 60 The pillar.

Fig. 61 The pillar.

Fig. 62 The pillar.

8. Gyrate Hips and Push Loins

Movements: (1) Gyrate hips: Continued from the previous posture. Move left foot half a step sideways, with width between feet a little more than that of the shoulders. With arms akimbo, turn hips clockwise 16 times, and counterclockwise 16 times (Fig. 63). Stand erect and bend forward and backward at the hip joints, 16 times (Figs. 64 and 65).

(2) Push loins: Continued from the previous posture. With arms akimbo, bend slowly forward at the waist to 90 degrees, and exhale. Jerk torso 4 times while exhaling. When you have exhaled to the full, raise torso slowly, and inhale. With thumbs as axes, turn fingers back, palms on sides of the small of the back. Bend torso back with force, and stare into the sky. Bob torso 4 times. When you have inhaled enough, slowly erect torso and return hands to commencing position. Do it 8 times (Fig. 66).

Essentials: While bending back, steady yourself on heels, with toes holding the ground. Drop vital energy to lower *Dantian*.

Effects: Exercising lumbar and hip joints, strengthening loins and kidney, preventing and curing backache.

9. Golden Rooster Stands on One Leg

Movements: With arms akimbo, straighten right leg, raise left leg and stretch it forward with instep straight tight, and kick 4 times. Stretch left leg back, instep straight tight, and kick backward 4 times with force (Figs. 67 and 68). Return left leg to forward position, turn left food in left circles 4 times and right circles 4 times, taking ankle as axis. Bend it down and kick back 4 times (Fig. 69). Return to original position. Reverse right and left, alternating 2 times.

Essentials: Stand fast with toes holding the ground. Concentrate your mind on ankle joint of the raised leg.

Effects: Exercising knee and ankle joints, strengthening legs and feet, preventing and curing rheumatic pain, numbness, and joint disturbances in lower limbs.

Fig. 63 Gyrating hips and
pushing loins.

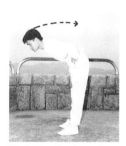

Fig. 64 Bending forward.

Fig. 65 Bending backward.

Fig. 66 Pushing loins.

Fig. 67 Golden rooster stands
on one leg.

Fig. 68 Golden rooster stands
on one leg.

Fig. 69 Golden rooster stands
on one leg.

10. Turn and Bend Knees

Movements: (1) Turn knees: Continued from the previous posture. Retrieve left leg, and close it with the right leg. Bend forward, hands on bent knees, and gyrate 8 times clockwise and 8 times counterclockwise (Fig. 70). Bend lower limbs 8 times (Fig. 71).

(2) Bend knees: Raise arms sideways to horizontal level, palms forward. Straighten legs and inhale. Drop arms to cross in front of abdomen while exhaling with bent knees. Take a short break after doing it 8 times. Do it again 8 times (Fig. 72).

Essentials: Stretch neck when bending forward. Make big circles of the knees. Keep your mind on both knees.

Effects: Strengthening the functioning of lower limbs and preventing and curing diseases in hips, knees and ankle joints.

Fourth Set   Principal Exercise – Lower Part

Commencing stance: Same as that for the first set.

1. Hold the Sky

Movements: Cross fingers in front of abdomen, raise hands, and inhale. When hands come to the chest, turn palms upward and hands continue raising. Eyes follow back of hands. Stretch hands to the full, and then lower them slowly. When arms become bent, raise hands again and do it 4 times. Inhale as much as you can. Part hands and exhale. Put down arms sideways, and cross fingers in front of abdomen. Do it 8 times (Figs. 73 and 74).

Essentials: Stand firm on heels, body erect, and use force to raise hands. Keep your mind on the three portions of the body cavity.

Effects: Regulating the three body portions, strengthening internal organs, and curing deformity of spinal column.

2. Draw the Bow

Movements: (1) Left bow: Move left foot a step to the left, bend knees, into horse-ride stance. Raise left arm sideways to horizontal level, palm forward. Strike left hand with right hand, inhale, and turn head to the left. Look to the left into the distance. Clench hands into loose fists, pushing with the left and pulling with the right. Incline torso the right to form right bow step. Pull with force 4 times with

Fig. 70 Turning knees.

Fig. 71 Bending knees.

Fig. 72 Bending Knees.

Fig. 73 Holding the sky.

Fig. 74 Holding the sky.

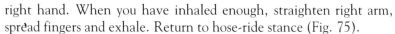

right hand. When you have inhaled enough, straighten right arm, spread fingers and exhale. Return to hose-ride stance (Fig. 75).

(2) Right bow: Reverse right and left. Do the exercise 4 times.

Essentials: Be steady with horse-ride stance. When drawing the bow, use force of the arms and other parts of the body. Draw it slowly, coordinating movements of hands, eyes, and torso, and combining mind, vital energy, and strength.

Effects: Expanding the chest, increasing volume of breathing, exercising shoulders, elbows and wrists, preventing and curing disorders of the heart, lung and joints of the upper limbs.

3. Raise Hand to Fix Spleen

Movements: Continued from the previous posture. Retrieve left and stand at attention. Throw out chest and draw in abdomen. Close hands in front of abdomen, left hand over right hand. Raise left hand to around the ear, fingers closed and palm up, pointing to the right. Inhale while raising left arm. Right hand presses down simultaneously, palm down and fingers pointing forward. Jerk hands several times. Inhale to the full and drop left arm slowly. Exhale. Slowly raise right arm. Close hands before the abdomen, right hand over left hand. Reverse right and left. Do the exercise 8 times (Fig. 76).

Essentials: Use force in pressing up and down. Keep your mind on spleen and stomach.

Effects: Regulating the spleen and stomach to guard against disease.

Fig. 75 Drawing the bow.

Fig. 76 Raising hand to fix spleen.

4. Look Back to Regulate Vital Energy

Movements: Continued from previous posture. Throw out chest, draw in abdomen, and thrust back shoulders. Keep torso steady, slowly turn head to back left, and inhale. Look back as far as you can. Inhale to the full, return head to original position and exhale. Reverse right and left. Do the exercise 8 times (Fig. 77).

Essentials: Keep torso steady when turning the head, and hands against thighs.

Effects: Exercising neck muscles, intensifying cervical vertebrae, stimulating blood circulation in the head, removing stagnancy in channels, tonifying the brain, preventing and curing hypertension and cerebral arteriosclerosis.

5. Glare and Thrust Fist

Movements: Continued from previous posture. Move left foot a big step to the side to form horse-ride stance. Clench hands into fists and place them by the waist, thumbs side up. Thrust left fist forward, turning thumb side down. Retrieve left fist. Reverse right and left. Thrust left fist to the left, and retrieve. Thrust right fist to the right, and retrieve. Do this exercise 8 times (Figs. 78 and 79).

Essentials: Thrust fist with force, with eyes following. Glare at the direction of thrust. Keep your mind on striking fist.

Effects: Exercising the arms, increasing body strength and stamina.

Fig. 77 Looking back to regulate vital energy.

Fig. 78 Forward thrust.

Fig. 79 Side thrust.

6. Touch Feet to Fix Kidney

Movements: Stand erect, with feet apart equalling width of shoulders. Raise arms forward and sideways, palms down, and inhale. Bend torso back, and look into the sky. Inhale as much as you can. Bend torso forward and drop arms, and exhale. Touch toes with hands, and jerk 4 times until you have exhaled. Erect torso, with arms following. Do it 8 times (Figs. 80 and 81).

Essentials: Stand firm, expand chest, and breathe deeply.

Effects: Exercising lumbar and abdominal muscles, strengthening cervical vertebrae, preventing and curing lumbar muscle strain, lumber spurs and kidney disorder.

7. Wag Tail to Strengthen Heart

Movements: (1) Wag tail and press leg: Continued from previous posture. Move left foot a setp to the side. Bend right leg to form horseride stance. Place hands on knees, with four fingers on one side and thumb on the other. Bend torso to front right, move hips to the left. Look at tip of left foot and press left knee with left hand 4 times. Swing hips to the right, look at tip of right foot, and press right knee with right hand 4 times. Alternate right and left 4 times (Figs. 82 and 83).

(2) Wag tail and beat leg: Assume right bow stance, holding right knee with right hand. Clench left hand, with thumb side towards leg. Starting from left hip, beat down the lateral side of left leg to ankle. Turn to the medial side, and beat up to base of thigh. Press left knee with left hand 8 times. Change into left bow stance and reverse right and left. Alternate 4 times. Return to the commencing stance (Fig. 84).

Essentials: Press and beat legs with force. Keep your mind on knee joints.

Effects: Exercising muscles of lower limbs, strengthening knee joints, promoting blood circulation, preventing and curing diseases of the heart and leg.

Fig. 80 Touching feet to fix kidney.

Fig. 81 Touching feet to fix kidney.

Fig. 82 Wagging tail to strengthen heart.

Fig. 83 Pressing leg.

Fig. 84 Beating leg.

8. Ride a Horse and Swing

Movements: Continued from previous posture. Erect torso, with arms bent by the side, thumb side opposite to each other. Lower hips into horse-ride posture, knees inside toes. Swing hands back and raise tips of feet. Swing hands forward, and place the tips on ground. Do it slowly 8 times, quickly 8 times, and again slowly 8 times. Return to the commencing stance (Figs. 85 and 86).

Essentials: Steady with your heels, keep torso erect and hips lowered, and finish it in continuous movements. Concentrate your mind on free end of the sacrum.

Effects: Vibrating gently joints in all parts of the body to guard against all kinds of diseases.

9. Eyes Follow Swinging Hand

Movements: Move left foot a step to the left, a little outside of the shoulder. Rest right hand on the hip, and raise left hand up before the eye, palm erect. Turn torso in large clockwise circles, 4 times. Eyes follow erect palm. Exhale when the torso is coming down, and inhale when it is up. Reverse right and left. Return to the commencing stance (Fig. 87).

Essentials: Keep legs straight. Turn torso slowly and gently in wide range. Lean back when turning up. Patients with hypotension and hypertension are prohibited.

Effects: Coordinating activities of all systems, balancing vital energy and blood, keeping body fit, and preventing and curing dizziness.

Fig. 85 Riding a horse and swinging.

Fig. 86 Riding a horse and swinging.

10. Roc Spreads Wings

Movements: Stand erect and cross arms in front. Exhale to the full, raise arms sideways, palms down, and inhale. When hands reaching the highest point, lift heels, and swing arms up and down. Inhale to the full, lower down arms slowly, and exhale. Heels touch ground. Return to original posture. Do it 8 times (Figs. 88 and 89).

Essentials: Do it in flowing movements. Be in cheerful mood. Have your mind on high above.

Effects: Strengthening body health, coordinating activities of the joints, and concluding the exercise in a calm mood.

Fig. 87 Eyes follow swinging hand.

Fig. 88 Roc spreads wings.

Fig. 89 Roc spreads wings.

Appendix: Location of Major Body Points

1. *Baihui*	2. *Tianmu*	3. *Zanzhu*	4. *Jingming*
5. *Yingxiang*	6. *Taiyang*	7. *Tinggong*	8. *Fengchi*
9. *Fengfu*	10. *Yamen*	11. *Zengyin*	12. *Laogong*
13. *Shenmen*	14. *Yongquan*	15. *Xuehai* (on medial side)	

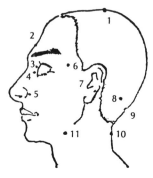 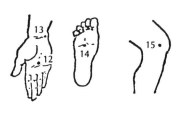

Fig. 90 Major body points.

1. *Qihai*	2. *Zhongfu*	3. *Dazhui*	4. *Shenshu*
5. *Mingmen*	6. *Huiyin.*		

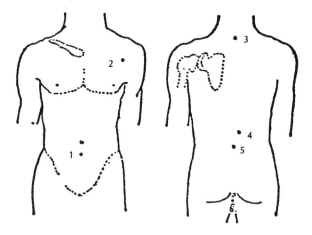

Fig. 91 Major body points.

Rejuvenesence Exercise

Rejuvenescence Exercise

Zhang Wenyi
Shanghai Research Institute of Traditional
Chinese Medicine

The rejuvenescence exercise, a type of the Chinses qigong, combines motion and stillness with motion sought in stillness and stillness sought in motion, and coordinates rigidity with suppleness. It is suitable to healthy people and people with light chronic diseases. It is especially good for wushu athletes.

The rejuvenescence qigong is divided into two parts: the principal part and the auxiliary part. The former is to build up a good foundation for people to do other exercises either for health-care or treatment of diseases of any kind. The latter consists of several different exercises which shall be adopted to suit individual physique, cases of diseases, and reactions from doing the exercises. This auxiliary exercise is used to strengthen effect of the principal part of rejuvenescence qigong to recover youthful vigor and fight against diseases.

The rejuvenescence qigong is a kind of keep-fit exercise of training the inborn vital energy. Its effectiveness will be doubled when combined with calming qigong. This is especially true with aged and weak people, since calming qigong nourishes the vital energy and produces inexhaustible vigor. The rejuvenescence qigong is also an exercise of training internally and externally, making the vital energy pass through all parts of the body with the function of preventing and curing diseases and dispelling the invading pathogenic factors by strengthening the patient's resistance. It can build up health, improve decrepit and atrophy condition, keep alive the fervour of youth and prolong life.

I. The Auxiliary Exercise

Standing Posture: Stand at ease with feet placed apart at the width of shoulders, and toes slightly pointing outward. Arms hang down. Relax your chest and shoulders, and hold your head straight and look forward. Imagine that a string attached to the top of your head is pulled tight from above. Your crotch is kept open with slightly out-bent knees, straight back, and drawn-in buttocks. Concentrate your mind on *Dantian*, slightly close your mouth, place your tongue against the palate, softly close your teeth, and breathe evenly.

Relax and attain tranquility. Relaxation starts with your head, from *Baihui* down to the neck, shoulders, chest, back, arms, epigastrium, the diaphragm, loins, the navel, lower abdomen, buttocks, thighs, knees, legs, ankles, and the soles of the feet. In short, make your whole body relaxed.

Draw your attention to *Dantian*. After a few minutes you feel *qi* (vital energy) at this point, a sensation of warmness from *Dantian*, numbness or itching. Sometimes your intestines gurgle. Your breath becomes even when you relax and attain tranuility. The rejuvenescence exercise uses paradoxical abdominal breathing. That is to draw in abdomen when inhaling and inflate it while exhaling. The breathing is to be kept in good rhythm – thin, deep, long, slow and even. Combine your mind with vital energy, i.e., guide the circulation of vital energy with your mind, from *Yongquan* via malleolus medialis, *Sanyinijiao*, *Yinlingquan* , *Yinlian*, perineum, *Changqiang*, *Mingmen*, and along the sides of the spine to *Dazhui* and *Baihui*.

While exhaling, guide the vital energy downward from *Baihui* to *Xiaguan* by the ears, and from the neck in two separate lines to *Quepen* and the breasts. Combine the two lines into one and send vital energy to *Zhongwan*, *Qihai* and the perineum. Split the line into two again and let vital energy get down to *Huantiao* on each side, *Fengshi*, *Yinlingquan*, external malleolus, *Kunlun* and back to *Yongquan*. This completes a cycle.

The time required for this exercise can be increased from 10 minutes to over 30 minutes. Never be in a hurry. But persistance will bring you satisfactory results.

II. The Principal Exercise

The rejuvenescence exercise prefers a piece of flat ground and a tranquil environment. If you do it indoors you have to leave the windows open to allow free air circulation. Face south or north.

Stand erect, feet shoulder-width apart. Arms hang down naturally. Hold head straight and look forward. Do not incline or recline body. Slightly close your lips with tongue lightly against the palate. Relax shoulders and draw in chest. Slightly bend your knees and loosen the joints all over your body. Concentrate on *Dantian*. This pile-stance is preparatory to the rejuvenescence exercise. Requirements: Relax your mind and body, use paradoxical abdominal breathing and breathe evenly and slowly for 1 to 2 minutes. Start with the following exercises when you have purged your mind of all distracting thoughts (Fig. 1).

1. Pushing the Bow Exercise

Stand with feet at shoulder width. Shift your weight onto your left foot with the right heel turning to the right. Move your weight onto the right leg. Raise left foot and move a step forward to get it into a T shape with the right foot. Shift your weight forward. Bend the fore leg and straighten the hind leg to form a bow stance. Place hands on *Shanzhong* on the chest, the left hand before the right hand, palms

Fig. 1   Fig. 2

Fig. 1 The principal exercise: Pile-stance.

Figs. 2-5 Pushing the bow exercise.

downward and slightly turned outward. The *Hukou* (area between the thumb and the index finger) of left hand rests exactly on *Shanzhong*, while the right middle finger points against the left *Hukou*. Describe clockwise a large circule and then a small one with both hands. Slightly withdraw hands. While shifting weight backward, move your hands to the right side of the lower abdomen (near the base of the hip). Turn right palm with *Laogong* upward and slightly close the fingers. Place left hand on right hand, palm down. Inhale slowly and draw in lower abdomen. Focus your mind on *Yongquan* and up to the malleolus medialis, right side of the lower abdomen, *Tianshu*, right ribs and *Jianjing*. While lifting your shoulders, straighten right leg, shift body slightly to the right, stretch right side of the back, and drag left foot back half a step (heel raised) to form a small T step. Turn right palm outward, push hand forward, and exhale. Move right foot half a step and turn torso to the front. Bend left leg and straighten right leg to form a left-bow stance. Turn right palm up and left palm around the tip of right elbow and downward, with left *Laogong* on right *Quze* (inside of the elbow). Withdraw right hand to the right side of the lower abdomen. Left hand comes down below the hip. Do this right-hand push three times and change to left-hand push. The movements are all the same except that the circles are to be done counterclockwise (Figs. 2, 3, 4 and 5).

Fig. 3

Fig. 4

Fig. 5

2. Bamboo Joint Exercise

Place feet at shoulder width. Shift weight to the left and move right foot forward half a step. Straighten the knee to form a T step. Lower your torso at the waist, with head lower than the crotch. Place right hand two *Cun* (6.6 cm) from the right external malleolus, and left hand two *Cun* (6.6 cm) from the right internal malleolus.

Inhale and wriggle your torso, with hands following it. Raise torso slowly. Move the vital energy from *Yongquan* to internal malleolus, *Sanyinjiao*, *Chengshan*, and *Weizhong*. When the vital energy comes to the back of the knee, lift hands to the side and exhale slowly. Then the vital energy returns via *Weizhong* along the same route to *Yongquan*. While the vital energy is travelling down, bend torso and lower hands rubbing and pushing. Stand still for a while. Again, guide the vital energy from *Yongquan* up to the internal malleolus, *Sanyinjiao*, *Chengshan* and back of the knee. During this course, wriggle your body dozens of times while inhaling. When the vital energy is coming down to *Yongquan* and you are exhaling, do the same number of wrigglings.

Continued from the previous stance. With right leg straightened, inhale to lift the vital energy via *Weizhong* to the inner side of the leg, the groin, *Yinlian* and *Huantiao* on the buttock. Lift hands and incline torso back, while the vital energy comes to *Huantiao* and down to *Yongquan*. Twist torso at the waist, and rub and push with the hands. Again, lift the vital energy from *Yongquan* via *Weizhong*, *Huantiao*, right side of the lower abdomen to *Shanzhong*. At this point, the hands have also reached *Shanzhong*. The body becomes erect.

Continued from the previous stance. Set the vital energy downward along the same route. Bend torso slowly until the vital energy reaches *Yongquan*. Stop for a while. Raise the vital energy from *Yongquan* via *Weizhong*, *Huantiao*, lower abdomen, *Shanzhong* to *Jianjing*. At this point, the two hands are placed before the collarbones. Slightly withdraw right shoulder. Stop for a minute. Draw in the right chest and send the vital energy from the right side to the left side of the chest. Push from the right side of the chest to its left side with two palms. Keep the vital energy in the left chest and erect torso. Shift weight forward. Left foot makes half a step to form a T shape. Left leg straightens while right leg bends. Send the vital energy from under the left *Jianjing* to *Wanzhong*, *Tianshu* and *Huantiao* on the left. Exhale during the time. Bend and twist towso and send the vital energy to left *Weizhong*. Bend left leg and move the vital energy down to *Yongquan*. Do this downward circulation of the vital energy three times with hands acting in good coordination. That means when the vital energy reaches *Yongquan*, do it twice more for it to go down from *Weizhong*. Lift the vital energy from right *Yongquan* to right *Jianjing* and left *Jianjing* and down to left *Yongquan*. This is the large cycle. Then, raise the vital energy from left *Yongquan* to left Jianjing. Right foot makes half a step. Send the vital energy to right *Jianjing* and right *Yongquan*. This is known as the left and right Bamboo Joint Circulation (Figs.6, 7 and 8).

3. Perineum Exercise

Place feet at shoulder width, with knees slightly bent. Calm down. Raise hands, palms up and middle fingers touching each other. Imagine that your are holding something in your hands. Inhale slowly and raise hands to guide the vital energy from *Yongquan* on both sides via inside of the feet to *Yinlian*. The two lines meet at the perineum and rise up to *Qihai* and *Xiawan*.

During the course, inhale 50 percent (never fully) and exhale one fourth while turning over the palms with middle fingers keeping touching each other. Hold the ground with your toes and use paradoxical abdomenal breathing. Draw in the abdomen while inhaling and lift the perineum. Guide the vital energy with mind from *Yongquan* to the internal malleolus and the perineum, and from the perineum into

Fig. 6

Fig. 7

Fig. 8

Figs. 6-8 Bamboo joint exercise.

the abdomen until it reaches the lower *Dantian*, *Zhongwan* and *Shan-zhong*. Your palms follow up to *Shanzhong*. Incline your torso at 30 degrees. Use your mind to guide the movement of the vital energy. For beginners the vital energy shall move to *Zhongwan* or *Jiuwei*. When they become skilled, they can guide the vital energy to *Shan-zhong* and *Tiantu* or even up to *Baihui*. You shall not overdo it to prevent any accident.

Turn over palms and push them down. The vital energy comes down step by step from *Shanzhong* to *Yongquan*. Imagine that it goes three *Chi* (100 cm) down into the earth. Exhale once whenever it goes down one *Chi* (33 cm). Relax toes when exhaling.

During the first cycle, inhale 50 percent and exhale one fourth. However, you breathe to the full during the second cycle to intensify strength of the mind (Figs. 9 and 10).

4. Liver-Gallbladder Exercise

Place feet at shoulder width. Move right foot forward half a step. Bend left knee, straighten right leg with heel raised. Stretch torso back, with hands rising to the right side of the upper abdomen, or the liver region. Describe nine clockwise circles with right hand, with fingers of left hand on its *Hukou*. Guide the right-left circular movement with your mind. Then, make nine counterclockwise circles with your left hand, rubbing from the upper left corner to the lower right corner.

Fig. 9

Fig. 10

Figs. 9-10 Perineum exercise.

The right hand moves accordingly. The hands are one *Cun* (3.3 cm) away from the abdomen. Then, pull and push nine times from the lower left corner to the upper right corner and vice versa, with your right hand to be supported by left hand. The same movement is repeated between the lower right corner and the upper left corner. After you finish rubbing, place left-hand fingers on right-hand fingers and lift and push down with the hands. Focus your mind on the right side of the abdomen to sense the vital energy churning up and down inside.

Lift and press nine times. Place the hands at level with the center of the right-side abdomen. Breathe with this part of the abdomen rising and falling. When rising, the hands move farther from the body, and when falling, they come closer. This is the right-side abdomen manipulation of the vital energy.

The left-side abdomen manipulation is the same. Move left foot half a step forwrd, with torso bent back. The movement of the hands is in the following sequence: (1) Clockwise circles; (2) Counterclockwise circles; (3) Rubbing from lower left to upper right; (4) Rubbing from lower right to upper left; (5) Lifting and pressing; (6) Rising and falling.

With *Zhongwan* as the center, do nine liftings and pressings, and risings and fallings. Stand at a natural pose.

The number of times varies in accordance with different situations. You can do the exercise by one nine times, or two and even four nine times. For people who are physically weak it is imperative to use the mind instead of breathing to the full (Figs. 11 and 12).

Fig. 11   Fig. 12

Figs. 11-12 Liver-gallbladder exercise.

5. Springing Exercise

Place feet as shoulder width. Raise right hand up to the waist, palm up. Raise simultaneously right foot three *Cun* (9.9 cm) above the ground. Keep the instep horizontal. Place left hand beside the left leg, palm down. The fingers of the two hands point forward. The left foot is slightly arched. Stretch right-side waist and relax the left-side. Stretch and bend the waist and knee two times. When bending, exhale with two pauses in between. Do not breathe to the full.

Right foot moves half a step, arches slightly, and touches the ground. Turn palm and press down to the full length of the arm. Raise left foot, with instep remaining horizontal. When bending and stretching the legs, the hands change position too. The left palm turns up, with the hand coming up to the waist. Slightly stretch and bend three times. Exhale in three parts. Then, move left foot half a step forward and repeat the whole precedure. Every time you finish a cycle you are a step forward. Focus your attention on *Dantian* and down to *Yongquan.*

Points to remember: When doing the bending and stretching relax every part of your body, the more the better. Inhale when moving foreard. Exhale when bending and stretching. Do not use force and do not use your mind. Everything goes on naturally. Imagine springs are fixed to your feet. You feel relaxed and comfortable after a few minutes. Guide the vital energy from *Dantian* to *Yongquan.* This exercise is beneficial to chronic diseases. It is also good for relieving accidental phenomena during the practice of qigong exercise, such as stuffiness in the chest and headache. It is a type of relaxing exercise (Figs. 13 and 14).

Fig. 13   Fig. 14

Figs. 13-14 Springing exercise.

6. Pacing like the Clouds Exercise

Stand with feet at shoulder width. Move weight to the left and crouch down slightly. Raise right foot 2-4 *Cun* (6.6 cm – 13.2 cm) above ground and move it to the right to make a circule. Return it to the left foot. Describe a similar circle with the right hand, palm down, at the same time. (The direction, position and timing of the movement of the hand and foot are identical.) Right foot makes a step forward to the right, with heel touching the ground first. While moving the right foot, slowly turn the right palm, with fingers pointing at the perineum, coming up from *Dantian* to the navel. Slightly draw in the abdomen and inhale. Turn from inhaling to exhaling when the heel touches ground and the body weight is moved forward. The vital energy expands from *Dantian,* with the abdomen rising. The right hand follows the movement of the right foot, and turn the palm slowly down. Bend right leg, and straighten left leg. Bend right leg and crouch. Raise slowly left leg and describe a circle toward left. Continue stepping forward (Figs. 15, 16 and 17).

Fig. 15   Fig. 16   Fig. 17

Figs. 15-17 Pacing like the clouds exercise.

7. Relaxing Exercise

Stand naturally with feet placed at shoulder width. Crouch slightly. Raise right hand slowly. Inhale, draw in the abdomen, and guide the vital energy to *Zhongwan*. Stretch the right-side waist and relax the left side. Turn up the right palm, by moving the little, third and middle fingers. Drop right hand from the waist to beside the leg while exhaling. The left hand rises simultaneously, fingers pointing forward, to the middle *Dantian*. Then, turn over the little, third and middle fingers of the left hand. Stretch left-side waist and relax the right-side. Drop left hand and raise right hand. This completes the whole cycle.

This exercise can be done either by standing at the same place or moving in lively steps. The vital energy is sent from *Shanzhong* to *Dantian, Huantiao*, by external route, *Chengshan, Zhuwai* and *Yongquan*. This is to be done on both sides of the body (Fig. 18).

8. Rubbing Exercise

(1) Rub the eyes with back of the thumbs to quench the fire of the heart, 16 times.

(2) Rub the nose with back of the tumbs to moisten the lungs, 32 times.

(3) Rub the ears with the thumbs and the foregingers to nourish the kidney, 16 times.

(4) Rub the face with the palms to strengthen the spleen, 32 times.

(5) Stop the ears with palms and drum with fingers the back of the head to clear the mind, 32 times.

Fig. 18

Fig. 19

Fig. 20

Fig. 18 Relaxing exercise.   Figs. 19-20 Rubbing exercise.

(6) Scrub *Yuzhenguan* with both hands to cure neurasthenia, 16 times each in clockwise and counterclockwise direction.

(7) Rub the small of the back with both palms to cure backache, 33 times.

(8) Rub the underside of the arch of feet to cure hypertension and insomnia, 16 times.

(9) Knock the upper teeth against the lower to relax the cerebral cortex and shake the nervous cells for good refreshing effect (Figs. 19 and 20).

(9) Closing Exercise

Stand naturally with feet apart at shoulder width. Arms hang down naturally, with kneen slightly bent. Left hand, palm facing up, rises from beside the leg to *Zhongwan*. Turn over the hand with the palm facing downward and lower it to the left side of the hips. Do it with the right hand as with the left hand. The exercise is alternately done sixteen times with two hands as if holding a ball before lower and middle *Dantian*. Inhale and the left hand is slightly placed on *Qihai*. Put the right hand on the left hand. While exhaling, move away the two hands from *Qihai*, with plams facing up. And then reverse right and left but after doing it sixteen times two palms facing up, with fingers to each other, rise slowly from lower *Dantian* to *Zhongwan* and inhale. While exhaling, turn over the two hands, palms down, and lower them to *Yongquan*. Do this rising and falling three times (Figs. 21, 22 and 23).

Fig. 21

Fig. 22

Fig. 23

Figs. 21-23 Closing exercise.

III Points to Remember

1. The exercise shall be taken at the place with fresh air. Stop doing it when you are in lower spirits.
2. Do the exercise every day. Be persistent and proceed along step by step. Do not be overanxious for success. Perseverance will bring you good results. When the vital energy is guided to the head, distension sensation in the head, throb of the temples, tinnitus, hyperscretion of eyes, thirst, thick coated tongue will occur. This is not strange. These phenomena will soon disappear with the further practicing the exercise. Whenever finishing doing the exercise, you will feel energetic and have a clear eye sight. It is not suitable for a patient with hypertension to guide the vital energy to the head.
3. Patients suffering digestive tract bleeding or spitting blood, apoplexy or severe diseases, who must lie in bed, are forbidden to do the exercise before recovery.
4. Do not do the exercise within half an hour after meal.
5. Sexual life must be controlled during the training.
6. Face the south or the north during the training.

Pile-Stance Qigong

Pile-Stance Qigong
– China's Popular Health-Care Exercise

Jiao Guorui

Pile-stance qigong (elementary) is an effective health-care exercise. It is easy to learn, requires no apparatus, and can be practised in the morning and evening and during work breaks. It relaxes the central nervous system, invigorates blood circulation and promotes metabolism. Pile-stance qigong keeps the body fit and cures and prevents many kinds of chronic diseases.

I. Essentials

1. Relax, be calm and natural. (1) During the exercise, relax not only your body but also your mind. Relaxation of mind is preliminary to that of the body. (2) Purge mind of all distracting thoughts to attain tranquility. Calmness of mind and body relaxation are interrelated to each other. (3) Be natural in posture, breathing and mind activities. Do this exercise without exertion.

2. Good posture. There are many postures. For instance, stand naturally with feet parallel to each other and apart at shoulder width. Rest body weight equally on both feet. Bend knees slightly and turn them a bit in. This is the requirements of lower limbs. There are also requirements of the torso (to be erect), of the chest and abdomen (to be drawn in a bit), of the head and neck (to be straightened) and of the mouth and eyes (to be levelled).

3. Make yourself comfortable. Be relaxed and calm, and do it naturally, and you will feel comfortable with correct posture. Never be rigid.

4. Advance step by step. The exercise shall be done in proper sequence and with great persistance. Impatience leads to bad results.

II. Methods

Pile-stance qigong can be divided into five types – the elementary, relaxing, high-posture, medium-posture and low-posture. The higher the posture, the lighter the load on the legs. Low posture increases the intensity. The following categories are good for the beginners.

1. Elementary postures

This type of exercise is suitable to all kinds of people except those who are extremely weak. It breaks down to the double posture and the single posture. The height of the posture is 10 centimeters shorter than that when you stand erect.

The double posture. Calm down, breathe naturally, with feet parallel and apart at shoulder width. Bend knees slightly and turn them in. Rest your weight on feet equally and squarely (never on heels) like deep-rooted trees. Stretch back and spine and relax the hips in a slightly seated posture. Relax shoulders, raise upper arms slightly from armpits, bend arms while hanging down naturally, and turn elbows slightly out. Hold head erect and stretch neck slightly back. Look squarely into the distance and breathe naturally. You will soon feel relaxed like a pine tree (Fig. 1).

The single posture. Place feet one after the other at 85 degrees. Rest 30 percent of your weight on the fore leg and 70 percent on your hind leg. The feet are one foot's or one and a half foot's length apart, with legs forming a "slightly seated bow stance". With knees slightly turned in, place feet firmly on ground like roots of a tree. The shoul-

Fig. 1

ders are relaxed. Alternate the left posture with the right. The other requirements are similar to those of the double posture (Figs. 2 and 3).

2. Relaxing posture.

This exercise has the slightest body load. It is the most suitable form for the aged and weak to begin with. Start practising other forms when you become stronger. There are many forms. Included here are the hand-in-pocket posture and hand-on-back posture. The relaxing posture refreshes the body and the mind. Its height is 5 centimeters lower than when you stand erect. This is why the load is lighter than that of the elementary postures.

Hand-in-pocket posture. Put hands in pockets to reduce the load on the shoulders. This posture can be done with the double or single posture. If you take the double posture, do everything according to the instruction of the double posture except that you put your hands in the jacket or trousers pockets with thumbs protruding. You are not to place the whole weight on the pockets to let your arms lie idle. For instance, you have to relax your shoulders, raise upper arms, bend arms and turn elbows out. After you become stronger you can practise other forms of the pile-stance qigong (Fig. 4). When you take the single posture, you put your hands in the jacket pockets (Fig. 5).

Fig. 2

Fig. 3

Fig. 4

Hand-on-back posture. In this posture the hands are placed on the back to reduce tension of shoulders and arms. In addition, your mind can easily be attracted to that part of the body to replenish function of the kidneys and invigorate the back and legs. You can practise it in the double or single posture. Take the double posture for example. Stand ready in accordance with the instruction. Place your hands on the back, with palms out, fingers pointing down diagonally and wrists on lower hip crests. Relax shoulders, bend arms, and erect torso. The shoulders incline slightly back without thrusting out the chest. The other requirements are similar to those of the double posture (Fig. 6). Again, take the right single posture for example. Move left foot one step forward to the left. Turn torso in the same direction. Shift weight onto the right leg. The hands on the back shall coordinate with the movement to balance the body weight and attain a good posture. The left single posture and the right single posture can be used alternatively. Other requirements are similar to those of the single posture (Fig. 7).

Fig. 5

Fig. 6

Fig. 7

3. High postures

This is the highest posture of all pile-stance qigong exercises. It is 10 centimeters shorter than your full length. It is similar to the elementary postures but 5 centimeters lower than the relaxing form. Therefore, the load is greater for the high postures. However, in high postures, the arms can be posed in many different ways. And the load, especially that on the arms, varies greatly. Generally speaking, the lower the posture of the hands, the lighter the load. When you begin, you begin with your hands at the lowest position. If you are weak but not too weak, you can start with high posture but low hand position. Following are three common types of high posture.

Down-press style. This can be practised with either double or single posture. Take the double as an example. Stand ready in accordance with instruction. Raise hands in an arc toward center and stop when they are at the level of the navel, palms down and slightly turned out. The fingers are spread apart and slightly bent. The thumbs are 15 centimeters away from lower abdomen. The fingers of the hands point to each other and are 30 centimeters apart. With elbows turning out, the hands are ready to press down (Figs. 8 and 9). The requirements of the mind and breathing are the same as those listed under the elementary exercise. In addition, try to imagine pressing movement of the hands. Light movements include "pressing ball in water" and "stroking ball in water." Heavy movements can be performed in the light of one's physical condition. However, the down-pressing imagination shall be

Fig. 8

Fig. 9

Fig. 10

slowed down at intervals so as to avoid rigidity. When you practise with the right single posture, you move left foot a step forward left, turn torso to the left, and shift weight onto right leg. The requirements of the arms are more or less equal to those for the double posture. But the left arm is a bit further forward, and the right arm a bit further back (Fig. 10). Alternate it with the left single posture.

Lift-and-hold style. It can be done with either the double posture or the single posture. Take the double posture for example. Stand ready in accordance with instruction. Raise hands in an arc to before lower abdomen, with palms turned obliguely in. The hands are 20 centimeters away from the body, with fingers spread and slightly bent. With fingers pointing to each other, the two hands are 30 centimeters apart, and are ready to lift and hold (Figs. 11 and 12). The requirements of the mind and breathing are listed under the elementary exercises. Besides, the mind shall be directed to imagine movements of lifting and holding. The light movements include holding a balloon. The heavy movements include holding a balloon. The heavy movements can be done according to one's physique. The lifting and holding shall be relaxed from time to time to prevent fatigue and rigidity. When you practise this lifting and holding with the right single posture, you move left foot a step forward left, turn torso left, and rest weight on right leg. The requirements of the arms are similar to those of the double posture, with left arm a bit more forward and right arm a bit backward (Fig. 13). Alternate it with the left single posture.

Fig. 11

Fig. 12

Fig. 13

Embracing style. It can be practised with the double or single posture. Take the double posture as an example. Stand ready in accordance with instruction. Raise hands before lower abdomen and up to the chest. They are at level with the breasts, palms inward, fingers spread apart and slightly bent. 20 centimeters apart, the fingers of the hands are pointing to each other. Imagine you are embracing a tree trunk (Figs. 14 and 15). Palms and wrists are pushing and pulling at the same time. Relax shoulders and elbows. The requirements of the mind and breathing are same with those of the elementary exercises. Imagine you are holding something. The light activities include embracing a balloon. The heavy ones can be executed in the light of one's physical condition. Relax the ideological activity at intervals to guard against fatigue and rigidity. When practising with the right single posture, move left foot a step forward left, turn torso left, and shift weight onto right leg. The requirements of arms are similar to those for the double posture. In addition, bend right arm in the form of a crescent, with hand at level with the breast and palm 30 centimeters away. Left arm forms a bow, with hand at level with the breast. Move left palm in front of the right, 20 centimeters apart. The body shall be in good coordination and good form.

Fig. 14

Fig. 15

Forward-push style. It can be practised with the double or single postures. In the case of the double posture, stand ready according to instruction. Raise hands before lower abdomen up to the chest. Turn palms obliquely out down. Keep hands at level with the breasts, fingers spread out and bent naturally. With fingers pointing to each other, the hands are 20 centimeters apart. Push out arms to form a ring. Imagine pushing forward with palms and wrists (Figs. 16 and 17). The requirements of the mind and breathing are the same with those of the elementary exercises. The imaginary activities are divided into two categories. The light movements include pushing at a balloon. The heavy movements can be done in the light of different physical conditions. Relax your mind from time to time to avoid fatigue and rigidity. When doing the right single posture, move left foot a step forward to the left, turn torso in the same direction, and rest weight on the right leg. The requirements of arms are similar to those of the double posture. However, left hand is moved forward, with elbow and arm extended to form a bow, while right hand is behind left, with thumb at level with the breast and away at a distance of two palm length. Relax shoulders and elbows. Keep body in a good form.

Fig. 16

Fig. 17

III. Points to Remember

1. Understand well the instructions and abide by the requirements. Be optimistic and practise them in an orderly way and step by step.

2. For beginners, do not mix the methods, requirements, mind activities and breathing of different exercises. Use the most simple method to begin with.

3. As health-care exercises, the pile-stance qigong can be done twice or thrice a day, each lasting 10 to 30 minutes. The duration can be increased step by step. Do not overexert. This is especially true for the weak people.

4. This exercise requires fresh air and a tranquil environment. If you are indoor, you need free flowing air. If you are outdoor, avoid scorching sunshine and cold winds. Keep away from the winds when you are sweating after the exercise.

5. Move the bowels and discharge the urine before exercising. Wear loose garments. Avoid practising on full or empty stomach. It is not suitable for beginners to do the exercise when they are tired. The exercise shall be done with a calm mind.

6. Return gradually to the normal state at the conclusion of the exercise. Do not stop abruptly, or you will feel uncomfortable.

目錄

三浴氣功

三 浴 氣 功

楊國權

一、功法特點

（一）　"三浴氣功"一詞解釋

三浴氣功屬中老年醫療保健功性質。

每天早晨，選擇陽光下、江畔湖邊、通風良好、空氣清新、負氧離子多的地方按氣功要領做功，進行光浴、水浴和氣浴。

（二）　"三浴氣功"的特點

（1）三浴氣功對身體各部都有不同程度的鍛煉作用。

（2）三浴氣功動作適合中、老年人的生理特點，整套動作符合人體生理機能活動變化的規律，生理負荷量中等。是用於防治疾病、增強體質的有效手段。

（3）三浴氣功的四套動作，可全做，也可選做。

（4）三浴氣功無特殊服裝、場地和氣候、地域要求，對男、女，老、中年，體質強、弱者都適宜。

（三）　"三浴氣功"的要領

（1）練功時要精神集中，排除雜念，以意念帶領做功，意、氣、力三者合一。

（2）練功時，呼吸要柔、勻、細、長，吸足呼淨，進行腹式呼吸（即以鼻呼吸，吸時自然凸腹，呼時自然收腹），氣貫丹田（臍下三寸）。

（3）注意控制動作的力量和速度。要全身鬆弛，用力適當，速度緩慢，循序漸進。

（4）注意動作的姿勢和節奏。要姿勢正確，節奏分明，弛張交替，有弱有強。

（四）　練功注意事項

（1）起床後要漱口，喝適量溫開水後再做功。

（2）不要在空氣污濁的地方做功。空氣過冷時，呼吸要慢而細或不做深呼吸。有烟、霧時禁做深呼吸。

（3）本功的第一套——按摩保健功，在冬季酷寒時，可在起床後或睡覺前於室內做，也可以在床上做。

（4）注意因人制宜，區別對待。慢性病發作期不做本功。恢復期做功宜先少做，再逐步增加，根據個人的體質和病情調整負荷量。患有高血壓、冠心病、腦動脈硬化和肺心病等症的練功者，做功動作不宜急驟，動作幅度不宜過大。

（5）要持之以恒。做到雨雪不誤，假日不停，堅持經常，才能使效果顯著。

（五）　"三浴氣功"的效果

可使病者康復，弱者轉強，健者延年益壽。

二、動作名稱

第一套　預備功——按摩保健功

（一）清心健腦　　　　（二）揉目擦臉

（三）揉太陽穴　　　　（四）浴鼻防感

（五）鳴鼓貫耳　　　　（六）叩齒鼓漱

（七）擦轉脖頸　　　　（八）推腹整腸

（九）擦腎健腰　　　　（十）擦腿挖脚

第二套　正功——上部

（一）白鶴亮翅　　　（二）餓虎撲食
（三）白猿獻桃　　　（四）順風掃葉
（五）前人指路　　　（六）雙龍盤柱
（七）海底撈月　　　（八）遙望三舍
（九）肺部療養　　　（十）騎馬呼吸

第三套　正功——中部

（一）天鵝騰空　　　（二）似上弓弦
（三）寬胸健肺　　　（四）摘星換月
（五）懷中抱月　　　（六）左右觀側
（七）朝天立柱　　　（八）轉髖托腰
（九）金鷄獨立　　　（十）轉膝屈伸

第四套　正功——下部

（一）雙手托天　　　（二）左右開弓
（三）單舉調脾　　　（四）後瞧理氣
（五）怒目衝拳　　　（六）攀足固腎
（七）擺尾强心　　　（八）騎馬顛擺
（九）觀手大轉　　　（十）鯤鵬展翅

三、動作說明

第一套 預備功——按摩保健功

預備式：心淨目潔，自然站立，肌肉放鬆，兩足同肩寬，十趾抓地。

（一） 清心健腦

動作：1. 搓髮：左手掌橫按前額，右手掌按後腦枕骨部，兩手稍用力，交叉回旋揉搓髮部。做16次（圖1）。

2. 撓髮：用十指指甲，由前頭部開始，按上、中、下三層，均勻地連續上下輕撓整個頭部的髮根。做2次（圖2）。

3. 捋髮：雙手掌按住前額，由前向後擦捋頭髮8次（圖3）。

要求：意念在頭頂百會穴。用力適度，呼吸自然。

作用：改善頭部神經的調節機能，清神健腦，使頭部皮膚增加活力，保養頭髮。

圖1 搓髮

圖2 撓髮

圖3 捋髮

（二） 揉目擦臉

動作：1. 揉目：雙目輕閉，用手掌小魚際處輕揉眼球，向左旋揉16次，向右旋揉16次，橫揉16次，上下揉16次（圖4、5）。

2. 擦臉：雙手掌由前額開始擦至下頷，再從下頷上擦，至耳輪處時，用拇指、食指擼擦耳輪，向上擦至頭後返回前額。做8次（圖6）。

3. 旋眼：兩眼輕閉，眼球用力左旋16次，然後兩眼慢慢睜開，平視遠望片刻；用同樣方法右旋16次，平視遠望片刻（圖7）。

要求：意念在雙目。擦臉時兩手用力要均勻。眼球旋轉要緩慢。遠望時要注目凝視不眨眼。

作用：豐潤面部皮膚，防治中、老年眼病。

（三） 揉太陽穴

動作：1. 揉太陽穴：雙手四指輕握，拇指用力按太陽穴，食指第二關節輕按攢竹穴，內外旋揉各16次（圖8）。

2. 捋眉弓：拇指按太陽穴不動，用食指第二節由前額天目穴擦至太陽穴16次，使天目穴開闊（圖9）。

要求：意念在太陽穴。閉目，按準穴位，輕旋，揉動均勻。

作用：清神明目。防治腦動脈硬化和中、老年性眼病。

（四） 浴鼻防感

動作：拇指微屈，四指輕握拳，用拇指背面沿鼻骨兩側，上至眼角，下至鼻孔側的迎香穴，稍用力往返擦16次。再用拇指指關節旋揉迎香穴，內外旋各16次（圖10、11）。

要求：意念在迎香穴。

作用：浴鼻通息。防治感冒、鼻炎、鼻竇炎和面神經麻痺。

圖4　揉目

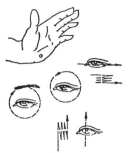

圖5　揉目位置圖

圖6　擦臉

圖7　旋眼

圖8　揉太陽穴

圖9　捋眉弓

圖10　浴鼻

圖11　揉迎香穴

（五） 鳴鼓貫耳

動作：1. 鳴鼓：兩手掌心緊按兩耳孔，中間三指交替輕擊後頭枕骨各16次（圖12）。

2. 貫耳：緊接上式，手指緊按後頭枕骨部不動，掌心按耳孔後再驟然抬離。做16次。

要求：鳴鼓時意念在腦戶穴，輕擊時應能聽到鼓鳴。貫耳時意念在鼓膜，動作稍用力，口微張。

作用：清醒頭腦，增強記憶，保護聽力。預防耳聾、耳鳴等老年性耳疾。

（六） 叩齒鼓漱

動作：1. 叩齒：口輕閉，兩手拇指分別按下頜兩側（增音穴），食指分別按左右耳屏（聽宮穴），中指分別按兩側太陽穴上，牙齒隨之開合。先輕叩門齒16次，再扣臼齒16次（圖13）。

2. 鼓漱：舌尖頂住上腭，鼓漱64次，待津液滿口後，分三次咽下（圖14）。

要求：叩齒時意念在下關穴，要逐漸用力。鼓漱時意念在舌尖。

作用：叩齒能使牙齒堅固，預防各種牙病。咽津能幫助消化食物，防治消化道疾病。

圖12 鳴鼓

圖13 扣齒

圖14 鼓漱

（七）　擦轉脖頸

　　動作：1.　擦頸：雙手放頸後，拇指在外與食指、中指共同捏住兩脖筋，由啞門穴起，至風府穴止，用力上捋脖筋16次。然後再下推脖筋16次（圖15）。然後左手按頸部右側，右手按頸部左側，由啞門穴到喉頭處，兩手交替揉搓脖筋。做32次（圖16）。

　　2.　轉頸：左手在下，右手在上（女則相反），使兩手勞宮穴（位於手心）重疊，按下丹田。頸部由左向右沿順時針方向緩慢旋轉8次（圖17）。再沿逆時針方向旋轉8次。然後頸部前屈、後仰8次（圖18）。

圖15　擦頸

圖16　搓脖筋

圖17　轉頸

圖18　前俯後仰

3.舒經：左手在下，右手在上（女則相反），虎口對準喉頭，開始吸氣，雙手用力向下推氣至下丹田，足跟提起，吸足氣後，足跟下落，開始呼氣，雙臂前後輕微擺動4次，將氣呼淨。做4次（圖19、20、21）。

　　要求：擦頸、轉頸時，意念在啞門穴。舒經時意守下丹田。

　　作用：疏通頭頸部經絡、血管。清心健腦。防治腦動脈硬化、高血壓等疾病。

圖19　舒經

圖20　舒經

圖21　舒經

圖22　推腹

（八） 推腹整腸

　　動作：1. 推腹：左脚向左前方邁出半步，身體隨之向左前方傾斜，兩手掌緊按肋下凹陷處，用力向前方推腹至臍部。然後，左手在下，右手在上（女則相反）使兩手勞宮穴重叠，用力推至下丹田。然後沿原路綫輕擦返回原處。做8次。然後左脚收回，改出右脚，身體向右前方傾斜，動作同前。做8次（圖22）。

　　2. 整腸：左手在下，右手在上（女則相反），使兩手勞宮穴重叠，緊按臍部，沿順時針方向旋轉揉擦小圈8次，再逐漸擴大至中圈8次，大圈8次。然後雙手上下交換，再沿逆時針方向，按大、中、小圈的順序各旋轉揉擦8次。做畢恢復預備式（圖23）。

　　要求：意念在下丹田。推擦要逐漸用力。孕婦、腹部患急性炎症和腫瘤者禁做。

　　作用：調理腸胃，助消化。防治各種胃腸和腹部疾病。

（九） 擦腎健腰

　　動作：用雙手背緊按兩側腰眼，用力下擦至尾閭處，然後再上擦至兩臂曲盡。做32次（圖24）。

　　要求：意念在腎俞穴（腰部）。

　　作用：强腰，健腎。防治腎臟疾病。對骨質增生、腰間盤突出等症有一定療效。

圖23　整腸　　　　　　　　圖24　擦腎

（十） 擦腿挖腳

動作：1. 擦腿揉膝：右腳向右側邁出一步，右腿彎曲，左腿伸直，成側弓步。右手掌按於右膝蓋上方，左手虎口向下，從左髖起，經腿外側用力向下推至踝關節處。轉手至內側，用力向上捋至大腿根，再沿腿根向斜上方捋至原處。做8次。緊接用左手掌按住髕骨，勞宮穴對準髕骨上緣，拇指按血海穴（腿膝關節處），向左旋轉8次，再向右旋轉8次。做畢，上體徐徐抬起（圖25）。然後呈左側弓步，左手掌按於左膝蓋上方，右手按上述左手動作。做8次。

2. 挖腳：自然直立，重心移向右腳，左腿伸直，左腳向右前方抬起。五趾先上翹再下挖，使湧泉穴（腳心）開闊。做8次。然後重心移向左腳，右腳按上述左腳動作。做8次（圖26）。

要求：推捋雙腿時意念在足三陽、足三陰。揉膝時意念在血海穴。挖腳時意念在湧泉穴。

作用：擦腿有助於下肢血液循環，疏通經絡。防治肌肉萎縮、靜脈曲張、下肢水腫、膝關節炎等疾病。挖腳可開闊湧泉穴。對高血壓、鼻塞不通、頭昏目花、老年足冷、下肢麻木等症均有一定療效。

第二套　正功——上部
預備式：同第一套

（一） 白鶴亮翅

動作：兩手輕握拳，雙臂伸直經前緩慢上舉，同時開始吸氣。舉至頭頂後，手指伸開，雙臂由體側緩慢下放，同時開始呼氣，手至體側，五指並攏，雙臂自然下垂前後稍擺動1次。做8次（圖27、28）。

要求：要深呼吸，氣沉至下丹田。足跟不要提起。

作用：疏通兩臂經絡，活動心肺，加速血液循環，強心健肺。防治肩關節功能障礙。

（二）　餓虎撲食

　　動作：兩臂自然下垂，由前向後繞，手至頭頂時上體緩慢後仰至極限，同時開始呼氣，兩手順勢前撲，手至足尖，五指抓攏。緊接上體徐徐抬起，同時開始吸氣，兩手握拳，拳心向上，兩臂隨上體抬起成前平舉，手指伸開，兩臂緩慢放下，恢復原式。做8次（圖29、30）。

圖25　擦腿

圖26　挖脚

圖27　白鶴亮翅

圖28　白鶴亮翅

圖29　餓虎撲食

圖30　餓虎撲食

要求：動作宜慢。呼吸時要吸足、呼淨。體前屈時幅度要大，腿要伸直。高血壓患者發作期禁做。

作用：鍛煉肩、腰肌腱，增強腰椎和肩關節的活動能力；促進胃腸蠕動。防治中、老年性肩、腰部疾病和胃腸疾病。

（三）　白猿獻桃

動作：兩臂自然下垂，兩手心向後，左腳向左側邁出一步，上體向左側轉，軀干伸直緩慢後仰，同時開始吸氣。隨之左腿伸直，趾尖抓地，右腿稍彎屈，兩臂屈肘徐徐做弧形上舉，雙手過頭，掌心朝天，指尖向後，雙目觀天，待氣吸足即甩手向下，同時開始呼氣，雙手返回原處，恢復原式。然後，右腳向右側邁出一步，上體右側轉，左、右腿分別按上述右、左腿動作，其餘動作同前。左右交替共做16次（圖31）。

要求：上體後仰時成背弓，重心在後側腿，力在腰、肩，氣沉下丹田。雙臂返回時要放鬆。

作用：活動兩肩和腰、髖關節。寬胸利膈，舒肝平胃。防治老年性脊椎彎曲和腰、背酸痛。

（四）　順風掃葉

動作：左腳向左側邁出一大步，兩臂伸直上舉，掌心向前，上體稍用力後仰，以腰爲軸，沿順時針方向緩慢旋轉，同時開始呼氣。上體轉至前下方時，指尖盡量靠近地面，待氣呼淨時，兩臂隨上體從右側緩慢向上旋轉，同時開始吸氣。將氣吸足後，手回至原處。旋轉8次。再用同樣方法沿逆時針方向旋轉8次（圖32、33）。

要求：兩腿伸直，十趾抓地站穩，兩臂保持肩寬。旋轉幅度要盡可能大，兩臂和上體運動要保持一致。意念要高遠。

作用：強腰補腎，活動全身。可預防頭暈。

（五） 前人指路

動作：雙手成劍指（食、中指伸出，餘三指虛握），兩臂自然下垂。左手沿順時針方向開始旋轉，轉至上方時，掌心向裏，轉至左側方時，掌心向外，眼看左手指尖。左手開始向下回原位時，右手沿逆時針方向開始旋轉至右側方時，眼看右手指尖。兩手左右交替，共旋轉16次（圖34）。

要求：眼隨指動，手眼合一。意念在劍指。

作用：活動上肢，增強視力。

圖31　白猿獻桃

圖32　順風掃葉

圖33　順風掃葉

圖34　前人指路

（六） 雙龍盤柱

動作：雙膝微屈，輕握拳，右臂屈肘，稍用力捶左前胸，同時左臂後伸，用左手背輕捶右側腰眼，收手時用左手手掌輕拍下腹部，右手手背輕叩命門穴，同時兩腿伸直。做8次。然後，左、右上肢分別按上述右、左上肢動作，其餘動作同前。做8次（圖35、36）。

要求：意念在中府穴。兩臂盤繞與膝部屈伸要協調。

作用：加強肩、肘、腕、膝關節活動。防治關節疾病和胸肋膜炎。

（七） 海底撈月

動作：左脚向左側邁出半步，兩臂伸直側平舉，彎腰向下，同時開始呼氣，雙臂由體側做弧形下落至足前，手指合攏成撈月式。然後上體抬起，兩手托捧至頭上，反轉掌心向下，兩手指尖及虎口相對，從胸前起緩慢下壓，同時開始吸氣，氣沉至下丹田。做8次（圖37、38、39）。

要求：動作要緩慢，呼吸要吸足、呼淨。

作用：加強腰關節和呼吸肌活動。防治腰椎骨質增生、胸膜炎及臟器疾病。

圖35　雙龍盤柱

圖36　雙龍盤柱

（八）　遙望三舍

動作：接上式，左脚再側出半步，雙手插腰，四指在前，拇指在後。上體向右方俯身，同時開始呼氣，至90°時以腰爲軸，緩慢向左側旋轉。旋轉時頭稍仰起，雙目掃視遠方。待頭轉至左方時，身體上抬，同時開始吸氣，上體後仰，眼觀天空，吸足氣。然後再沿原路綫返回，按上述動作，次序相反。做8次（圖40、41）。

要求：雙足站穩，轉動緩慢，極目遠望，吸足呼淨。

作用：調節目力，强腰，健肺。防治近視、花眼、迎風流淚。

圖37　海底撈月

圖38　海底撈月

圖39　海底撈月

圖40　遙望三舍

圖41　遙望三舍

（九）　肺部療養

動作：接上式，左脚收回一步，雙手插腰。從左肩開始向上、前、下、後方勻速旋轉。左肩開始向下時，右肩隨之向上，做同樣動作。做16次後稍停，再從右肩開始，按上述動作，做16次。雙手放下，恢復預備式（圖42）。

要求：以雙肩的運動帶動肺部活動。雙肩旋轉時腰部不要隨之轉動，意念在雙肩。

作用：增强肩關節活動能力，促進肺部活動。防治肺部疾病。

（十）　騎馬呼吸

動作：接上式，兩足尖內收成倒八字，兩臂伸直前平舉，兩手半握拳，拳心向下，屈膝下蹲成騎馬式，同時開始徐徐吸氣。身體輕微上、下顫顫數次，待氣吸足後身體緩慢起立，同時開始呼氣。雙臂自然下落，前後輕微擺動數次，待氣呼淨後，再重複做一次。做畢恢復預備式（圖43、44）。

要求：成騎馬式時上體垂直，膝蓋不超過足尖。氣沉下丹田。

作用：活動腰、髖、膝、踝關節。疏通經絡，調動眞氣，有健身作用。防治腰腿酸痛等症。

圖42　肺部療養

圖43　騎馬呼吸

圖44　騎馬呼吸

第三套　正功——中部

預備式：同第一套

（一）　天鵝騰空

動作：1. 騰空：兩臂於腹前交叉，雙膝微屈，同時開始呼氣。呼盡後雙膝伸直，兩臂伸直側上舉，同時開始吸氣，雙手在頭上靠攏，兩手勞宮穴重疊後，兩臂由體側自然放下，至腹前交叉，做8次（圖45、46）。

2. 飛躍：緊接前式，兩臂側上擺，掌心向下，開始吸氣，同時左腿側擺，右足跟提起。隨之兩臂放下，開始呼氣，左腿收回。然後，右腿側擺，左足跟提起，其餘動作如前，交替共做16次（圖47、48）。

圖45　天鵝騰空

圖46　天鵝騰空

圖47　飛躍

圖48　飛躍

要求：騰空動作舒展稍慢，呼吸深、細、稍快，飛躍動作連貫自然。意念高遠，心曠神怡。

作用：活動四肢關節，鍛煉四肢肌肉。調節神經，愉悅心境，協調全身運動。

（二） 似上弓弦

動作：接上式，雙手翻掌向前，兩臂前斜下舉，十指自然彎屈，開始吸氣，上體緩慢用力大幅度後仰，成背弓形。隨之兩臂由下經後向上繞舉，至頭頂時，身體緩慢直起並稍前傾，開始呼氣，兩臂從前方徐徐下落至原處。做8次（圖49、50）。

要求：上體後仰時，要十趾抓地，雙足站穩。氣沉下丹田。

作用：舒筋活血，鍛煉肺部，增強腹背肌力。防治老年性脊柱彎曲。

（三） 寬胸健肺

動作：接上式，手指微屈，上體前傾90°，含胸，同時開始呼氣。隨之兩臂側下伸成摟抱形，待氣呼淨後，兩臂隨上體緩慢抬起，同時開始吸氣。上體直立時雙手向側下後方擴胸展臂，上體隨之後仰，手至側下方時將氣吸足。做8次（圖51、52、53）。

要求：以擴胸為主。動作緩慢，雙足站穩。氣沉下丹田。

作用：舒展胸廓，鍛煉呼吸肌。強心健肺。

圖49　勢上弓弦

圖50　勢上弓弦

86

（四） 摘星換月

　　動作：雙手插腰，左脚側出一步成左弓步。隨之上體左轉，左臂伸直放下，五指伸開，從側前方向上旋轉。手至頭上時，五指捏攏，左臂從側後方旋轉回原處，手指伸開。做16次（圖54 ）。然後兩腿伸直，身體隨之轉向正前方，左手由左下方經體前向右上方旋轉，同時吸氣，手至頭上時五指捏攏，然後左臂經原路綫返回，同時呼氣，手指伸開，掌心向後。做16次。

　　再換右側弓步，上體分別右轉及正向，右上肢按上述左上肢動作，其餘動作同前。做16次（圖55、56 ）。

　　要求：意念在五指，眼隨手動。

　　作用：活動肩、肘、腕、指關節。防治上肢末稍震顫、麻木和肩周炎。

圖51　寬胸健肺

圖52　寬胸健肺

圖53　寬胸健肺

圖54　摘星換月

圖55　摘星換月

圖56　摘星換月

（五）　懷中抱月

動作：接上式，兩手勞宮穴相對，作抱球狀，兩臂向左上方做弧形推送，上體順勢向左上方向探出，隨之右足跟提起，重心移向左腿。然後按上述方法向右側做，左足跟提起，重心移向右腿。左右交替，共做16次（圖57）。

要求：意念在勞宮穴。眼隨手動。動作舒展飄逸，推送幅度要大，稍用力。手要保持抱球狀。

作用：活動四肢及全身肌內。強心，健身。

（六）左右觀側

動作：接上式，左脚收回半步略比肩寬，雙手正插腰，上體緩慢前傾成90°，同時開始呼氣，上體向下點動四次，待氣呼淨後抬起，同時開始吸氣，上體左側屈，隨之右臂經體側上舉至頭上時，屈肘掌心向上，雙眼順肩下視左足跟，上體向左下方點動四次，待氣吸足後，身體回正，雙手恢復正插腰。然後上體右側屈，左臂按上述右臂動作，雙眼按上法視右足跟，上體向右下方點動4次。左右交替共做4次。做畢恢復預備式（圖58、59）。

要求：體前屈、側屈時用力要緩，膝要伸直，氣沉下丹田。

作用：鍛煉肋間肌、腰肌。強健脾胃。

圖57　懷中抱月

圖58　左右觀側

圖59　左右觀側

（七） 朝天立柱

動作：接上式，雙手正插腰，身體垂直上挺，雙足跟抬起，同時開始吸氣。隨之雙手掌心朝地，指尖向前，用力下壓，足跟用力柱地，開始呼氣，將氣呼淨。做8次（圖60、61、62）。

要求：全身用力向上抻拔。氣沉下丹田。足跟落地時要稍用力，使腦部有輕微震動感。

作用：抻拔全身韌帶，行氣通脈，强身，健腦。

圖60　朝天立柱　　　圖61　朝天立柱　　　圖62　朝天立柱

（八） 轉髖托腰

動作：1. 轉髖：接上式，左脚側出半步，略比肩寬，雙手正插腰，以髖關節爲軸，沿順時針方向旋轉16次；再按逆時針方向旋轉16次（圖63）。然後身體直立，以髖關節爲軸，前俯、後仰交替，共做16次（圖64、65）。

2. 托腰：接上式，兩手正插腰，以腰爲軸，上體緩慢前俯90°，同時開始呼氣。呼氣時上體點動4次。待氣呼淨後，上體徐徐抬起，同時開始吸氣。以拇指爲軸四指轉向背後，掌心托住腰眼，上體用力大幅度後仰，雙目觀天，利用脊柱反彈力振動4次，待氣吸足後，上體徐徐直起，雙手恢復正插腰。做8次（圖66）。

要求：托腰後仰時，要足跟站穩，十趾抓地。氣沉下丹田。

作用：活動腰、髖關節，強腰健腎。防治腰部酸痛。

（九） 金鷄獨立

動作：兩手正插腰，右腿直立，左脚抬起，向左前方伸出，脚背綳直，彈踢4次後，左腿收回向後伸，脚背綳直，用力向後蹬伸4次（圖67、68）。隨之左腿回至左前方，以踝關節爲軸，左旋轉4次後，右旋轉4次。接着踝關節用力背屈（足伸）向足跟方向用力踏蹬4次（圖69）。然後恢復正插腰，左腿直立，右下肢按上述左下肢動作做。左右交替，共做2次。

要求：支撐脚五趾抓地站穩。意念在非支撐脚的踝關節。

作用：活動膝、踝關節，強腿健足。防治下肢風濕疼痛、麻木和關節不利。

圖63　轉籠托腰

圖64　前俯

圖65　後仰

圖66　托腰

圖67　金雞獨立

圖68　金雞獨立

圖69　金雞獨立

（十）　轉膝屈伸

動作：1. 轉膝：接上式，左腿收回，兩腿並攏。上體前屈，兩手扶膝，兩膝彎屈，按順時針方向旋轉8次；沿逆時針方向旋轉8次（圖70）。然後下肢再屈伸8次（圖71）。

2. 屈伸：兩臂側平舉，掌心向前，兩腿伸直，同時開始吸氣，兩臂下落至腹前交叉時雙膝微屈，同時開始呼氣。做8次後稍停，再做8次（圖72）。

要求：上體前屈時，頸部要伸直。兩膝旋轉的幅度盡量要大。意念在雙膝。

作用：增強下肢功能。防治髖、膝、踝關節疾病。

第四套　正功──下部

預備式：同第一套

（一）　雙手托天

動作：雙手在腹前十指交叉上托，同時開始吸氣，手至胸前翻掌繼續上舉，眼看手背，用力托舉至極限。然後雙手緩慢下降，待臂稍屈再徐徐用力上托，連續向上托舉4次。待氣吸足後，雙手分開，同時開始呼氣，兩臂由體側緩慢放下，手在腹前十指交叉，做8次（圖73、74）。

圖70　轉膝

圖71　屈伸

　　要求：足跟站穩，身體挺直。雙手上托時要用力。意念在三焦。

　　作用：調理三焦，強壯臟腑。矯治脊柱彎曲。

圖72　屈伸

圖73　雙手托天

圖74　雙手托天

（二） 左右開弓

　　動作：1. 左開弓：左脚向左邁出一步，兩腿屈膝下蹲成騎馬式。左臂側平舉，掌心向前，右手經體前扣擊左手，開始吸氣。同時頭向左轉，眼順左手方向遠望。雙手半握拳成拉弓式（左推、右拉），身體隨之右傾成右弓步，右手用力顫拉四下，待氣吸足後，右臂伸直、舒指，開始呼氣，恢復騎馬式（圖75）。

　　2. 右開弓：左、右肢體分別按上述右、左肢體動作做，其餘動作同前。左右開弓各做4次。

　　要求：騎馬式要蹲穩。開弓時兩臂、全身都要用力。緩慢將弓拉開，做到手、眼、身協調，意、氣、力合一。

　　作用：擴張胸廓，加大肺呼吸量。活動肩、肘、腕關節。防治心、肺和上肢關節疾病。

（三） 單舉調脾

　　動作：接上式，左脚收回成立正式，挺胸收腹，雙手在腹前合掌，左手在上。左臂伸直上舉附耳，五指並攏，掌心向上，指尖向右。左臂上舉時開始吸氣，同時右手掌心向下，指尖向前，用力下按。雙手自然顫動數次，待氣吸足後，左臂緩慢下落，開始呼氣，同時右臂緩緩抬起，右手在上，雙手在腹前合掌。然後左、右上肢分別按上述右、左上肢動作，其餘動作同前，左、右交替，共做8次（圖76）。

圖75　左右開弓

圖76　單舉調脾

要求：上舉、下按要同時用力。意念在脾胃。

作用：調理脾胃。防治脾胃疾病。

（四）　後瞧理氣

動作：接上式，挺胸，收腹，兩肩稍向後引。上體不動，頭緩慢向左後方轉動，同時開始吸氣，雙眼盡量向後瞧，待氣吸足後，頭緩慢回正。同時呼氣，將氣呼淨。然後，頭緩慢向右後方轉，其餘動作同前。左、右各做8次（圖77）。

要求：轉頭時上體不動，雙手靠腿。

作用：鍛煉頸部肌肉，增強頸椎活動，改善頭部血液循環。舒經健腦。防治高血壓、腦動脈硬化。

（五）　怒目衝拳

動作：接上式，左腳側出一大步，成騎馬式，兩手握拳抱於腰間，拳心向上。左拳由腰間向前用力衝出，同時拳心轉向下。將左拳收回抱於腰間，用同樣方法衝出右拳。然後將右拳收回抱於腰間，左拳向左衝出。左拳收回抱於腰間，右拳向右衝出。做8次（圖78、79）。

要求：衝拳時要用力，手眼相隨。兩眼怒視拳擊方向。意念在衝出拳。

作用：鍛煉臂力，增強身體的力量和耐力。

圖77　後瞧理氣

圖78　前衝拳

圖79　左右衝拳

（六） 攀足固腎

動作：直立，兩足同肩寬。兩臂經前至側上舉。兩手掌心向下，同時開始吸氣，隨之上體後仰，雙目觀天。待氣吸足後，上體緩緩向前深屈，兩臂隨身體下落，開始呼氣，兩手觸摸足趾，上下點動4次，待氣呼淨後，上體緩緩直立，臂隨之上舉。做8次（圖80、81）。

要求：站穩，擴胸，深呼吸。

作用：鍛煉腰、腹肌，強健腰椎。防治腰肌勞損、腰椎骨質增生和腎臟疾病。

（七） 擺尾强心

動作：1. 擺尾壓腿：接上式，左腳側出一步，右腿屈膝成騎馬式。手扶同側膝，虎口向下，上體向右前方前俯深屈，臀部向左擺出，眼看左足尖，左手用力按壓左膝4次。然後臀部向右擺出，眼看右足尖，右手用力按壓右膝4次。左、右交替共做4次（圖82、83）。

2. 擺尾捶腿：右側弓步，右手扶右膝，左手握拳，拳心向腿，由左髖部開始，沿腿外側依次向下捶打至踝部。再從內側由下而上依次捶打至大腿根部。再用左手用力按左膝8次。然後成左側弓步，左手扶左膝，右手握拳，分別按上述右、左手動作。左、右交替共做4次。做畢恢復預備式（圖84）。

要求：壓腿、捶腿要用力。意念在膝關節。

作用：鍛煉下肢肌肉，增强膝關節功能，促進血液循環。防治心臟、腿部疾病。

圖80　攀足固腎

圖81　攀足固腎

圖82　擺尾強心

圖83　左右壓腿

圖84　左右捶腿

（八） 騎馬顛擺

動作：接上式，上體挺直，屈臂在腰間，拳心相對，臀部後坐，膝蓋不超過足尖，成騎馬式。手向後擺，同時足尖抬起，手向前擺，同時全腳掌着地。慢做8次後，快做8次，再慢做8次。做畢恢復預備式（圖85、86）。

要求：足跟站穩，上體挺直，臀部後坐，動作連貫。意念在尾閭。

作用：輕微振動全身各關節。有消除百病之功效。

（九） 觀手大轉

動作：左腳向左邁出一步，兩足寬於肩，右手正插腰，左手成立掌上舉至眼前。以腰為軸，上體沿順時針方向大幅度緩緩旋轉4圈。旋轉時眼看立掌。向下旋轉時呼氣，向上旋轉時吸氣。然後左手正插腰，換右手成立掌，其餘動作同前，做畢恢復預備式（圖87）。

要求：兩腿伸直。上體旋轉時速度要慢，幅度要大，動作要柔和。上旋時身體稍後傾。高血壓、低血壓病患者發作期禁做。

作用：協調全身系統活動，平衡周身氣血，強健全身。防治眩暈。

圖85　騎馬顛擺　　　　圖86　騎馬顛擺

（十） 鯤鵬展翅

動作：直立，兩臂體前交叉，將氣呼淨後，兩臂側上舉，掌心向下，同時開始吸氣，手舉至最高點時，足根提起，兩臂上、下輕微擺動作飛翔式。待氣吸足後，雙臂緩慢下落，開始呼氣，足根着地，恢復原式。做8次（圖88、89）。

要求：動作舒展大方，心情愉快，意念高遠。

作用：強健身心，協調關節活動。結束全功。恢復安靜。

圖87　觀手大轉

圖88　鯤鵬展翅

圖89　鯤鵬展翅

附：主要穴位圖

1、百會 2、天目 3、攢竹 4、睛明 5、迎香 6、太陽 7、聽宮 8、風池 9、風府 10、啞門 11、增音 12、勞宮 13、神門 14、湧泉 15、血海（裏側）

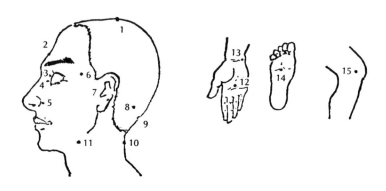

圖90 主要穴位

1、氣海 2、中府 3、大椎 4、腎俞 5、命門 6、會陰

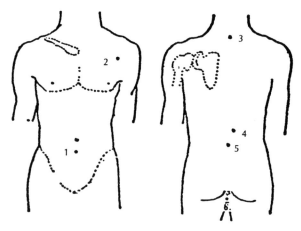

圖91 主要穴位

返還功

返 還 功

"返還功"，古稱"却老術"，有返本還原之意。

這種氣功有動有靜，動中有靜，靜中有動；可剛可柔，剛柔相濟。既適於一般健康的人，也適於病情較輕的慢性病患者習練，並特別適於練武術的人操練。

本氣功分：主要功法和輔助功法。所謂主要功法是指無論爲了保健或防治疾病，亦不分何種病症，都由此開始打好練功的基礎，再練其它功法；輔助功法則是按照各人體質、病情和在練功中產生的各種變化等具體情況，分別運用不同的練功方法，以輔助和加強主要功法的作用，起到返老還童，對抗疾病的效果。

返還功是鍛煉人的元氣，是一種健身術。我們練返還功，配合靜功，能起到事半功倍的效果。尤其年老體弱者，由於適當利用安靜來滋養元氣，使之元氣充沛、精力旺盛。再加上返還功能使氣遍身軀，是內修外練的一種功，起到能防病治病、袪邪扶正之作用。即《內經》的所謂"正氣內存、邪莫能干"。該功能增強體質，改善人的衰老痿退狀態，使之長葆靑春、延年益壽。

一、輔助功法

站式：我們以自然站立爲佳，兩足與肩同寬，兩足尖微向外撇，成小八字步。兩手自然下垂，沉肩含胸。眼向前平視，頭放正，頂勁虛靈領起。兩膝微曲，腰要直，臀要收，襠要開。（兩膝蓋向外略撇，襠就開圓。）氣沉丹田，口輕閉，舌輕抵上腭，齒輕合，調息綿綿。

掌握上式要領後，隨即鬆弛入靜。從意識上，由頭部先放鬆，從百會而下，經頸項、肩、胸、背及手臂，到上腹、兩肋部橫隔膜、兩腰，下至臍，隨後放鬆小腹、臀部，最後，由大腿、膝蓋、小腿、足踝至足底及全身放鬆。

先意守丹田，到一定時候自然能得氣。一般會出現丹田發熱、腸鳴蠕動、發麻，或發癢，如蟻行或熱流。如能做到靜、鬆、自然，就可調息。我們練返還功，採用逆式腹呼吸法。吸氣時收腹，呼氣時腹部隆起。呼吸要有節律，在鬆靜的基礎上要注意到：細、深、長、慢、勻五個字。意氣結合，即由意識導引氣的運行。由湧泉經足內踝，上三陰交、陰陵泉，直上陰廉、會陰，循長強至命門、夾脊而上出大椎至百會。

隨着呼氣，由百會向下導引，從左右落至兩耳邊的下關，由頸而下，兩綫分開。從缺盆向下送，至兩乳，再合二爲一至中脘，入氣海、會陰。再向外側分兩綫至環跳，下達風市、陰陵泉，經足外踝，由昆侖入湧泉爲一周。

每次練的時間，由十分鐘漸至半小時以上。不要操之過急，只要持之以恒，久而久之，自能水到渠成。

二、主要功法

練返還功法，最好是選平整的場地，環境要安靜。如室內要開窗，保持空氣流暢。面向南或北。

身體要正站立，兩足與肩相寬。兩臂自然下垂。頭部正直，雙目平視。不要前俯後仰。唇輕閉，舌抵上腭，不要着力。肩要鬆而下沉，含胸拔背，兩膝微曲，全身各關節放鬆，意存丹田。站樁就是做返還功前的預備功法。要求：神舒體靜，採用逆式腹呼吸法。呼氣時要勻、緩、細、長。凝神靜息一至二分鐘，覺得心無雜念，呼氣綿綿，吸氣微微時，即可練下列功法（圖1）。

（一） 弓推運氣法

兩足自然站立，與肩寬。重心左移。右腳跟原地向右撇後，重心移於右腿。提左腳向前邁開一步，成丁字形，重心前移。弓前腿，後腿撐直，成弓步。同時，兩手由下而上，皆會於胸前膻中穴前。左手在前，右手在後。兩手掌心朝下，略向外撇。左手虎口對準膻中，右手中指尖對準左手虎口。接着，雙手同時順時針方向，畫一大圈，再畫一小圈。然後，兩手略向內收，在重心漸漸後移的同時，至小腹右側（近胯根外）。右掌心漸翻轉，使勞宮穴向上，五指微並攏。（收勞宮穴）左手在右手之上，左掌心向下。接着，緩緩吸氣，小腹漸收，意識由湧泉經足內踝向上至小腹右側，經天樞、右肋而上，直至肩井。提肩的同時，右腿漸伸直，身微右移，右腰拔長，左腳隨勢拖回半步，（足跟點起）成小丁字形步。接上式，右手掌外翻，漸向前推手，同時呼氣。右腿邁出半步，身體漸漸轉正。弓左腿，右腿直，成左弓步。接上式，右掌心漸轉向上，左掌心由對右肘尖漸向上翻，掌心轉向下，（勞宮對曲澤）對右肘節彎處。右手向下、向內回收，至小腹部右側，在手落至胯下，繼續再做第二次右推手，一共做三次。再換左弓推手運氣法。動作如同右側，畫圈改為逆時針方向（圖2、3、4、5）。

圖1　主要功法：站樁

圖1

圖2─5　弓推運氣法

圖2

圖3

圖4

圖5

（二）　竹節運氣法

　　兩足站立與肩相寬，重心左移，右脚向前邁開半步，膝蓋伸直勿曲，成丁字步。接上式，俯身彎腰，頭部朝下低於襠。右手在右足外踝旁二寸左右處。左手在右足內踝旁二寸左右處。

　　繼上式，慢慢提氣，在吸氣的同時，上身前後左右扭動，兩手亦隨着擺動，一上一下地提引，上身漸升起。意識由湧泉起，經內踝至三陰交，過承山入委中。當氣引至膝膕內，兩手亦上引至膝蓋兩側，隨後慢慢吐氣。再由委中往下送，經原路至湧泉。上身亦隨着下氣而俯身，兩手也搓推而下。稍停，再由湧泉復內踝而上，復三陰交、承山再次入膕。從湧泉至委中，腰要扭動數十次，邊扭動，邊吸氣，邊上升提氣。下放呼氣亦是如此。

　　繼上式，右脚仍伸直，吸氣上提，由委中經大腿內側，直上腹股溝、陰廉處，再橫向後至環跳。兩手亦隨着上提，上身繼續仰起，當氣提至環跳時，再又由環跳往下送氣至湧泉。同時腰部扭動，兩手搓推。再由湧泉提氣，逐節而上，過委中、環跳，經右側小腹，直至膻中。此時，兩手掌亦提至膻中。身體已直立。

　　接上式，按以上的要求的運氣路綫，繼續向下送氣，俯身而下，直至湧泉。稍停，繼從湧泉提氣。通過委中經環跳，再會於小腹。由小腹經膻中直上肩井，此時，兩手掌亦置於鎖骨前，右肩略向後收。稍停，含右胸，氣由右胸送至左胸。兩手掌從右胸推送至左胸，左胸亦含氣身正。繼之，重心前移。左脚復上，跨出半步成右丁字步。左腿伸直勿曲，右腿微下蹲。繼上式，將左胸肩井下之氣向小腹送去。此時，漸漸吐氣，從脘中直送至小腹天樞，及左腿環跳。俯身扭腰，繼續往下送，直至左脚委中。此時可以曲左腿，再由委中往下送氣，直至湧泉。這樣由兩手配合着往下連送三次。當氣達湧泉時，再從委中往下送氣三次。由右脚湧泉拔氣至右肩井，再轉運至左肩井，直下送左脚湧泉為一大循環。做完上式後，再由左足湧泉提氣至左肩井。右足上半步，通過右肩井復送至右足湧泉，為左右竹節運氣。又謂之階梯運氣法。主要是逐步逐節的運氣（圖6、7、8）。

圖6—8　竹節運氣法

圖6　　　　　　　　圖7　　　　　　　　圖8

（三）　會陰升降運氣法

　　兩足與肩同寬，膝蓋微曲，站立寧神。兩手由下往上抄，掌心朝上，兩手中指尖相對，如托物狀。緩緩吸氣，兩手隨勢上托提氣。意識由湧泉穴拔氣上提，經兩足內側至陰廉，復會陰，將會陰元氣上提入腹，至氣海、下脘即可。

　　自湧泉至下脘，吸二分之一的氣，（不要吸足）接着，慢慢吐氣，兩手掌翻轉，中指相對，掌心皆朝下，隨着降氣下推，只吐氣四分之一。足趾要抓地，以逆式腹呼吸法。吸氣時收腹，提會陰。用意識將氣由湧泉，經足內踝直提至會陰入腹，由下丹田上至中脘，入膻中。兩手掌亦隨之提到膻中。身體要向前傾三十度。練時要貫串意識，通過意識來帶動氣的運動。初練時，只可引氣至中脘或鳩尾。待功夫純熟了，可拉至膻中或天突，甚至可拉到百會穴。初練時，切不可勉強，以防衝氣出弊。

　　繼之，再反掌。漸漸下推，氣由膻中逐節下送至湧泉穴。意念之氣由湧泉穴入地三尺。每入一尺，吐一口氣。吐氣時，足趾放鬆。

　　在做第一次呼吸時，先以二分之一吸氣進提法，吐氣時，只吐四分之一。做完第一次後，第二次則用強呼吸，即加強了意識的力量（圖9、10）。

（四）　肝膽運氣法

　　兩足與肩寬。右脚向前邁開半步，左膝曲，右脚伸直，足尖踮地，上身向後仰。兩手同時上提，在右上腹部，即肝區範圍，以右手為主，左手指貼於右手虎口，由右至左畫圈。意識帶動右上腹旋轉，順轉九偶。繼之，再逆轉九圈。轉時以左手為主，由左上角向右下角來回搓擦，右手跟着擺動，兩手離腹約一寸許。全憑意念帶動搓擦九個來回。再以右手為主，左手為輔，由左下角向右上角拉推，同樣來回九次。然後再從右下角向左上角拉推九個回合。搓擦完，左手指搭在右手指上，兩手上下提推。意識右側腹內，氣上下滾動，如海豚式的呼吸法，起伏蠕動。

繼上，九次上下滾翻後，兩手搭在右腹中間，護右腹一收一隆。隆起時，兩手也稍離開腹部，當收縮時，兩手也向腹部靠近，這是右側腹部運氣法。

左側上腹運氣法亦和右側相同。即左足跨出半步，上身後仰。手的動作分：（1）順轉，（2）逆轉，（3）左下向右上搓擦，（4）右下向左上搓擦，（5）翻滾法（亦稱一上一下），（6）一隆一縮，即合緊弛（亦稱一前一合）。

接着，以中脘爲中心同樣做上下翻滾九個回合，再做一前一後（一隆一縮）的動作。兩脚以自然站立即可。

每次練時，可做一九數，即每次九數如九轉，也可做二九或四九，主要看每人的素質和健康狀況而定。如身體較差的，可用意念，而不用强呼吸（圖11、12）。

圖9—10　會陰升降運氣法

圖9

圖10

圖11—12　肝膽運氣法

圖11

圖12

（五） 蹲跳步法（又名：彈跳步法）

兩足與肩相寬，右手由下而上提，掌心朝上，與右腰齊。同時右足亦隨着提起，約三寸高，足背平。（足尖不上翹，足跟不後提）左手掌心向下，落於左腿旁，兩手指尖皆朝前。左足着地微曲。右腰拔長，左腰鬆弛下沉。腰與膝微微伸曲，隨着鬆抖二伸二曲。在曲的同時，呼氣三下。也就是一氣分三次呼，不必吸足呼完。

右足跨半步，微曲着地。同時，掌心轉向下壓，至手直伸爲度。左腿跟上提起，腳背平。在二足曲伸時，兩手要隨一上一下。左手心由下而翻轉朝上，並向左腰側提上，輕輕抖動三下。呼氣分三吐。隨後，左足向前，邁開半步，繼續一上一下，升降開合，周而復始，做一次上一步。氣沉丹田，直至湧泉。

該功法要點是：在做提抖動作時，要全身放鬆，越鬆越好。在進步時，轉換吸氣；鬆抖下沉時，呼氣。不要用力，也不要用意識，隨其自然，腳上如安置彈簧。練過幾分鐘後，自覺鬆弛、舒暢，氣沉丹田，入湧泉。對慢性病患者有較好的效果。對於氣功弊病，如胸悶、頭脹，亦能顯著轉機。這是一種行之有效的放鬆功（圖13、14）。

圖13—14　蹲跳步法

圖13

右腳

圖14

左腳

（六）　踱雲步法

　　兩足站立與肩同寬，重心左移，身微下蹲。右足輕輕提起，離地約二至四寸，然後向外右分，畫一圈，再至左脚旁。在畫圈的同時，右手亦隨着右足的方向畫一圓弧。掌心朝下。（注意：手與足的方向、位置、起落是一致的）右足再向右前方邁開一步，足跟先着地。在右足起步的同時，右手掌漸翻，指尖對準會陰，自下而上，經丹田至神闕，腹略收，吸氣。當足跟着地，重心前移時，由吸氣轉爲呼氣。氣由丹田而出，腹漸隆起。右手隨着右足，掌心漸翻轉朝下。弓右腿，左腿撑足。復上式，右足弓步下蹲；隨勢，左足慢慢提上，向左分弧形畫成一圈。繼續邁步向前（圖15、16、17）。

圖15—17　踱雲步法

圖15　　　　　　　　圖16　　　　　　　　圖17

（七）　放鬆活步法

　　兩足自然站立，與肩同寬。身微下蹲。右手慢慢由裏向上。吸氣收腹至中脘。右腰拔長，長腰胯下沉。掌心轉向上。由小指、無名指、中指漸轉漸翻，向右腰側翻掌，掌心朝下，慢慢吐氣，右手漸漸下沉，落於腿旁。掌心由腰下沉的同時，左手漸漸上提，手指皆朝前，至中丹田處，隨後，左手小指、無名指、中指漸轉漸翻。左腰拔長，右腰胯下沉，掌心旋轉向下，右手掌慢慢向上提，左右周而復始。

　　該功法練時，即可站立原地，又可用活步前進，升降開合。氣由膻中至丹田，外側入環跳、承山、足外、湧泉穴。左右皆同（圖18）。

（八）　神衰磨擦法

1. 拇指背拭目，去心火。做十六次。
2. 拇指背擦鼻，潤肺。做三十二次。
3. 拇指、食指擦耳，補腎。做十六次。
4. 左右掌心擦面，健脾。做三十二次。
5. 雙手掩耳，鳴天鼓，清頭腦。做三十二次。
6. 左右手搓玉枕關，治神經衰弱。順做十六次，逆做十六次。
7. 左右掌擦腰眼，治腰痛。做三十三次。
8. 摩擦左右足心，治高血壓、失眠。做十六次。
9. 叩齒。通過上、下牙齒抖動，放鬆大腦皮層，震盪神經細胞，得到充分休息（圖19、20）。

（九）　收功法

　　自然站立，兩腳與肩相寬。兩臂自然下垂，雙膝微曲，第一次，先左手，後右手掌心向上，從左側大腿旁緩緩上提至中脘前。開始漸漸翻手，掌心向下，徐徐下放至左側腰胯處。接着右手如同左手一樣上提下放，交叉循環進行，如抱球狀，在下、中丹田前反覆來回十六個回合。此時，隨着吸氣，左手輕輕地覆蓋在氣海穴，然後，右手也緩緩地合在左手上。待呼氣時，二手即離氣海穴，掌心皆向上。緊接着做第二次，先右手，後左手，其動如同左手一般，但在上下循環交叉來回十六個回合後，兩手掌心皆向上，五指相對從下丹田處緩緩上提（吸氣）至脘中穴前，然後兩手漸漸朝裏向下翻，掌心皆向下（呼氣），徐徐下放至湧泉穴。這樣上提下放來回循環需要做三個回合。也叫做三個開合（圖21、22、23）。

圖18　放鬆活步法　　　　圖19—20　神衰磨擦法

圖21—23　收功法

三、注意事項

1. 練功地點必須選擇空氣新鮮之處。心情不佳時，可暫停練功。

2. 堅持天天鍛煉，持之以恒，日久自然見效。循序漸進，逐步提高，不可操之過急。當氣提到頭部時，可能會出現頭脹、太陽穴跳動及耳鳴等，有時會出現眼分泌物增多，口干，舌苔厚等現象，這並不奇怪。隨着練功的進行會很快消失而恢復正常。每當練完功後會覺得眼目清亮、精神充沛。但對於高血壓患者則不宜把氣提到頭部。

3. 有消化道出血，吐血，中風及較嚴重疾病而臥病在床患者，未愈前禁止練功。

4. 飯後半小時內，禁止練功。

5. 必須節制性生活。

6. 練功時，注意朝南北方向練。

站 椿 功

站 椿 功
——我國民間的一種保健醫療運動
焦國瑞

　　站椿功（初級功）是一種有效的保健醫療運動，優點是，簡便，不需任何練功設備，利用早晚或休息時間都可進行鍛煉。它的作用，不但能使中樞神經得到休息，還能加強血液循環，促進新陳代謝，對保健强身和防治多種慢性病都有很好的效果。

一、站椿功的鍛煉要領

　　站椿功（初級功）的基本要領有以下幾點：

　　（一）鬆靜自然。它包括三個內容：第一，是放鬆。練功時不僅肢體要放鬆，精神也要放鬆，因爲只有精神不緊張了，肢體才能放鬆。第二，是寧靜。練功時要排除雜念，使精神活動進入到相對安靜的狀態。對於鬆與靜只是要求在鍛煉時，肢體能够相對地放鬆，精神能够相對地寧靜。放鬆可以幫助入靜，入靜又可以幫助放鬆。第三，是自然。這是指練功的許多方面說的，諸如姿勢、呼吸和意念活動，在鍛煉時都要力求自然，不可過於勉强，所謂練功之道，法於自然，就是這個道理。

　　（二）體式完整。這是對練功體式（姿式）提出的要求。站椿功有許多種體式。例如，身體自然站立，兩脚平行分開，與肩同寬，兩脚平均着力，兩膝微曲、稍向內扣，兩髖內合等，這是對下肢的要求。還有對軀幹的（上體正直）、對胸腹的（如含胸收腹）、對頭頂的（如項背挺拔）、對口眼的（如正頭平視）各項要求。

　　（三）舒適得力。這是指進行鍛煉時的自身感覺。要作到這一點，首先就要作到鬆靜自然、體式完整。練功貴於自然，切不可過於呆板。

（四）循序漸進。練功應該按照一定的要求、方法、要領，循序漸進，勤學苦練，持之以恒。心情急躁，急於求成，非但對功夫長進無益，而且往往會適得其反。

二、站樁功的練功方法

站樁功的體式可分爲基本式、休息式、高位式、中位式和低位式五大類。體式越高，身體的支撐量越小；體式越低，身體的支撐量越大，鍛煉的強度也就越大。這裏僅就基本式、休息式和高位式中適合於初學站樁功的幾種體式介紹如下。

（一）基本式

只要不是身體過於虛弱的人，都可從基本式練起。基本式有雙重基本式和單重基本式兩種。這種體式的高度，比直立時降低一拳左右。

雙重式：練功時，寧靜心神，自然呼吸，身心放鬆；兩脚平行分開，與肩同寬；兩膝微曲，稍向內扣；兩脚平均着力（避免體重落在脚跟），如樹生根；腰脊豎直，舒放挺拔；兩髖內合，臀部稍呈坐勁；鬆肩虛腋，兩臂微曲，自然下垂，肘臂稍向外撐；正頭平視，項背微同後撐。兩眼平視遠方，呼吸力求自然，細心體會練功時身體產生的輕鬆舒適的感覺，意如蒼鬆之屹立。練功家所謂站如鬆，即爲此意（圖1）。

圖1

單重式：兩脚一前一後斜向錯開呈85度，前脚着力輕，後脚着力重，前、後脚着力之比，一般爲三與七之比。前後脚之距離，約爲一隻脚或一隻半脚的長度，下體呈"小坐弓步"體式。兩膝稍向內扣，兩脚如樹生根，肩架勻稱，體式完整。左重式與右重式調換鍛煉。其他要求均同雙重基本式（圖2—3）。

（二）休息式

這是站椿功裏身體支撐量最輕的體式。年老體弱，在初學時可先從休息式練起，待身體逐步好轉後，再練其它體式。休息式有很多種，這裏只介紹插兜式和貼腰式兩種。休息式對消除體力和腦力疲勞有很好的作用。體式的高度，比直立時降低半拳，所以，此式比基本式的身體支撐量爲輕。

插兜式：此種體式是借助於將手插在兜內以減輕肩臂支撐量的體式。可以練雙重式，也可以練單重式。以雙重式爲例，按雙重基本式要求站好，將兩手插在上衣兜內或褲兜內，大指露在外邊。其它要求均按雙重基本式鍛煉。插兜式雖借助衣兜的荷重，可以減輕上肢的支撐力量，但也不可將肩臂的支撐力完全放在衣兜上，以免失掉上肢的鍛煉作用。衣兜只起減輕的作用，上臂仍須根據自己的體力，對鬆肩虛腋、曲肘撐臂進行鍛煉，待體力增強到一定程度時，即可改練其它體式（圖4）。練單重式時，按單重基本式要求擺好體式，只是把兩手插在衣兜內，其他要求除參照雙重插兜休息式外，均按單重基本式要求鍛煉（圖5）。

貼腰式：此式是借助於將兩手反貼在腰部以減輕肩臂支撐量的體式，同時由於兩手背反貼在腰部，練功者的意念活動也就很自然地有一部分要注意到腰部的穴道上，所以此式也有補益腎氣、強健腰脚的作用。可以練雙重式，也可以練單重式。以雙重式爲例，按雙重基本式要求站好，將兩手反貼在側腰部（手心向外，手指斜向後下，以手背的基底部貼於髖峭的後下部），鬆肩曲臂，上體正直，兩肩作整體性的微向後引，（但不要挺胸）注意肩架勻稱，體勢完整。其它要求可按雙重基本式要求鍛煉（圖6）。練單重式時，按單重基本式要求站好。以右重式爲例，左脚向左前方上一步，身體順勢稍向左轉，重心落於右腿，貼於側腰部之兩手要與全身的力量作一整體性的移動，以求全身力量和體式結構之完整舒適。左重式與右重式，調換鍛煉。其他要求可參照單重基本式（圖7）。

圖2

圖3

圖4

圖5

圖6

圖7

（三）高位式

這是站樁功中體式較高的一類姿式。體式高度比直立時降低一拳，與基本式相同，比休息式低半拳。所以，高位式的支撐量，比休息式支撐量大，但由於高位式的上肢有許多不同的體式，所以身體的支撐量、特別是上肢的支撐量有很大差別。一般地說，手的位置越低，其負重量越小，手的位置越高，其負重量越大。所以，練高位式站樁時，就其循序漸進來說，也是從手的低位體式開始的。身體不太虛弱者，都可從高位式低手位練起。高位式的體式很多，下面介紹三種比較常用的體式。

下按式：可以練雙重式，也可以練單重式。以雙重式為例，按雙重基本式要求站好，將兩手自兩髖外側向中間畫弧緩緩上提於小腹之前，手與臍平，掌心向下，稍向外展，五指分開，略微屈曲，大指與小腹相距約一拳半左右，兩手指尖相對，相距約三拳左右。肘臂稍向外撐，兩手作下按式（圖8—9）。意念與呼吸，除按基本式要求鍛煉外，意念活動主要是體會作下按鍛煉時產生的舒適感覺。下按時的意念活動與力量，有輕有重，輕的意念活動，猶如“水中按球”或“水中撫球”，所以，此式也叫按球式或撫球式；重的意念活動可根據自己的體力情況，“加大”下按的意念活動。作下按的意念活動時要有鬆緩的間歇，以免過勞或僵緊。作單重鍛煉時，按單重基本式要求站好。以右重式為例，左腳向左前方上一步，身體稍向左轉，重心落在右腿。上臂要求同雙重下按式，但左臂略向前移，右臂稍向後撤，全身體勢作一整體性的改變（圖10）。左重式與右重式調換鍛煉。

提抱式：可以練雙重式，也可以練單重式。以雙重式為例，按雙重基本式要求站好，將兩手自兩髖外側畫弧緩緩上提於小腹之前，掌心斜向內上，手與小腹相距約兩拳左右，五指分開，略微屈曲，兩手指尖相對，相距約三拳左右，兩手作“提抱勁”（圖11—12）。意守與呼吸，除按基本式要求鍛煉外，意念活動主要是體會作"提抱"鍛煉時產生的舒適感。提抱的意念活動，有輕有重，輕的意念活動，猶如提抱一個"氣球"；重的意念活動，可按照自己的體力情況適當加大提抱的意念活動。作提抱意念活動時要有鬆緩的間歇，以免過勞或僵緊。作單重鍛煉時，按單重基本式要求站好。以右重式爲例，左腳向左前方上一步，身體稍向左轉，重心落在右腿。上臂要求同雙重提抱式，但左臂略向前移，右臂稍向後撤，全身體勢作一整體性的改變（圖13）。左重式與右重式調換鍛煉。

圖8

圖9

圖10

圖11

圖12

圖13

環抱式：可以練雙重式，也可以練單重式。以雙重式爲例，按雙重基本式要求站好，將兩手自兩髖外側經小腹前方緩緩抬至胸前，兩手與乳平高，掌心向內，五指分開，略微屈曲，兩手指尖相對，相距約兩拳左右。兩臂如作環抱樹幹之勢（圖14—15），腕掌稍作外撐內抱，肩肘略作下沉。意守與呼吸，除按基本式要求鍛煉外，意念活動主要是體會作環抱鍛煉時全身產生的舒適感。環抱之意念活動有輕有重，輕的意念活動，猶如環抱一個氣球，重的意念活動可據自己的體力情況適當加大。作環抱意念活動鍛煉時要有鬆緩的間歇，以免過勞或僵緊。作單重鍛煉時，以右重式爲例，左脚向左前方上一步，順勢身體稍向左轉，重心落在右腿。上臂要求同雙重環抱式，右臂環抱，形如半月，手與乳平，掌心與乳相距約爲三拳；左臂如弓背，手與乳平，左掌在右掌之前，相距約兩拳許，體式務求完整協調。

圖14

圖15

前撐式：可以練雙重式，也可以練單重式。以雙重式爲例，按雙重基本式要求站好，將兩手自兩髖外側經小腹前方緩緩抬至胸前，掌心斜向外下，與乳平高，五指分開，略微作屈曲，兩手指尖相對，相距約兩拳左右，兩臂外撐如環形，腕掌作前撐勁（圖16—17）。意守與呼吸除按基本式要求鍛煉外，意念活動主要是體會作前撐鍛煉時全身產生的舒適感。前撐之意念活動有輕有重，輕的意念活動，猶如撐按在一個氣球上，重的意念活動可根據自己的體力情況適當加大。作前撐鍛煉時，意念活動應有鬆緩間歇，以免過勞或僵緊。作單重鍛煉時，以右重式爲例，左脚向左前方上一步，身體順勢稍向左轉，重心落在右腿。上臂要求同雙重前撐式，只是左手前移，肘臂外撐如弓，右手在左手之後，拇指平乳，相距約兩掌，肩肘略作下沉，全身務求舒適得力。

圖16

圖17

三、鍛煉時的注意事項

（一）對練功要認眞領會練功要領，遵守練功注意事項，堅定信心，循序漸進。

（二）初學的人，不要把幾種不同的功法、要求、意念活動和呼吸方法，自行混雜在一起鍛煉，以免產生流弊。在練功方法上，初學者總是以簡爲妥。

（三）作爲一般的保健鍛煉，在練功次數和時間的掌握上，一般地可以一日練二、三次，每次練10—30分鐘。時間應逐漸增加，不可過力，不可勉強延長時間。應在質量上下功夫。體弱者尤須避免過力。

（四）練功環境，最好在空氣清新和比較安靜之處。室內練功，要空氣流通。室外練功，要避免炎日照曬，冷風吹襲。練功出汗後，不可當風着涼。

（五）宜在功前排除大小便，衣服、領扣和其他束緊處應放鬆。不要在過飽或有饑餓感時練功。初學者也不宜在過勞時鍛煉。練功時應保持心情平靜。

（六）練功結束時，要作好"收功"。方法是使身體從練功狀態逐步回復到平時狀態而不要猛然地收功，這樣會使身體感到不舒適。